CAMBRIDGE
UNIVERSITY PRESS

Cambridge Lower Secondary
Global Perspectives

Keely Laycock

CAMBRIDGE
UNIVERSITY PRESS

Shaftesbury Road, Cambridge CB2 8EA, United Kingdom

One Liberty Plaza, 20th Floor, New York, NY 10006, USA

477 Williamstown Road, Port Melbourne, VIC 3207, Australia

314–321, 3rd Floor, Plot 3, Splendor Forum, Jasola District Centre, New Delhi – 110025, India

103 Penang Road, #05-06/07, Visioncrest Commercial, Singapore 238467

Cambridge University Press is part of the University of Cambridge.

It furthers the University's mission by disseminating knowledge in the pursuit of education, learning and research at the highest international levels of excellence.

www.cambridge.org
Information on this title: www.cambridge.org/9781108790543

First published 2020

20 19 18 17 16 15 14 13 12 11 10 9

Printed in the Netherlands by Wilco BV

A catalogue record for this publication is available from the British Library

ISBN 978-1-108-79054-3 Paperback

Additional resources for this publication are available through Cambridge GO. Visit www.cambridge.org/go

⟩ Contents

Section 4: Reflection

Section 5: Collaboration

Section 6: Communication

〉 Introduction

Global Perspectives is all about helping you to develop a range of important skills that will aid you not only in your school and academic life but also in your future career. For example, in any job it's likely that you'll need to *collaborate* with others and of course you'll need to *communicate* when doing this. Getting a job might seem a long way off now, but even at school, working well with your classmates is really important. For example, when carrying out a science experiment or preparing a group presentation about a piece of literature. As you get older, you will increasingly be asked to *reflect* on how well an activity or a piece of work has gone. In studying Global Perspectives, you learn how to develop these really important practical skills as you explore fascinating topical issues and learn about different points of view from around the world.

This Learner's Skills Book follows on from Learner's Skills Book 7 and is designed so that you can continue to develop skills in research, analysis, evaluation, reflection, collaboration and communication as well as to understand what is meant by each of these terms. As in the Learner's Skills Book for Stage 7, each skills section follows the same approach, guiding you through a 'Starting with', 'Developing' and 'Getting better at' scaffold, building your awareness of your progress and allowing you to take charge of your own learning journey. A range of activities and tasks is included, with plenty of opportunities for peer-to-peer and group work, and to enable you to reflect on your progress, track your achievements and record your next steps.

The learner's skills books for Global Perspectives 7–9 are write-in resources, so you can create and keep a portfolio of your work and track your progression through each skill and each stage as you head towards the Checkpoint assessment at the end of Stage 9. When responding to the Independent reflection activities at the end of each lesson and to the Self-assessment activities to set learning targets, I encourage you to take the time to answer these questions about your own learning as honestly as possible. Being aware of how you learn will help you to learn more effectively, and this will be a very valuable skill for you to have.

I hope that you will continue to enjoy exploring a wide range of global topics and discovering different viewpoints from around the world – these, and the skills you will learn and develop, will equip you in countless ways – in school, in your career and in your life.

Keely Laycock

How to use this book

This book contains lots of different features that will help your learning. These are explained below.

These are the learning objectives that will be covered in each lesson. ⟶

> **1.3** Select an appropriate method and conduct research to test predictions and begin to answer a research question
>
> **1.4** Select, organise and record relevant information from a range of sources and findings from research, using appropriate methods

This list sets out what you will learn in each lesson. You can use these learning goals to identify the important topics for the lesson. ⟶

My learning goals are to start to:

- recognise that some facts in a news story might not be true
- identify bias in a source
- realise that news stories may contain bias
- realise that the argument in a source should make sense if it is to be trusted

This will help you to know when you have met your learning goals. ⟶

How will I know if I reach my goals?

As you work through this lesson and you achieve your learning goals, tick the 'Achieved' box to show you have completed this. If you haven't quite achieved your learning goals, tick 'Not there yet'. Start to think about how you are going to show your learning goals in your challenge. Add an example from your challenge once you have achieved each learning goal.

Lesson 3	Not there yet	Achieved	Example
I know some ways of telling whether facts in a news story are untrue.			
I can identify bias in a source.			
I realise that news stories may contain bias.			
I realise that the argument in a source should make sense if it is be trusted.			

These are questions or tasks to help check your level of understanding before beginning a lesson. ⟶

Prior learning

1 How do you check if information that looks like a fact in a source is real or fake? Discuss with a partner.

....

2 Check with another pair. Do they agree or have different ideas?

....

Each tip provides useful information and key points to consider. ⟶

Tip

An unreliable source is a source that cannot be trusted to be true.

This focuses on how you are learning, rather than what you are learning, and you can set yourself learning targets for the next lesson/s.

Independent reflection activity

Which part of today's lesson did you find the most difficult?

....

Why do you think this was?

....

What skills have you used today?

....

These are check-ins at the end of each lesson, to encourage you to reflect on your progression through the learning goals, and relate this to your Challenge topic.

Check your learning

If you haven't already done so, complete the **How will I know if I reach my goals?** table with 'Not there yet' or 'Achieved'. Don't forget to add examples from your challenge.

This allows you to consider your progress through the learning goals. The red-amber-green checklist encourages you to think about where you are on your learning journey, and to look back at past self-assessments to see clearly how you are progressing.

Self-assessment 3

Look back at self-assessments 1 and 2. How much further progress do you feel you have made so far in developing your reflection skills?

For each learning objective in the table below, shade in the response that matches yours most closely. Give one example for this response. Eventually, you are aiming for green!

Learning objectives: *to get better at . . .*	RED	AMBER	GREEN
4.1 Explain personal contribution to teamwork and identify targets for improvement.	I can explain how I contribute to teamwork, referring to my personal strengths. I can explain some targets for improvement with help.	I can explain how I contribute to teamwork, referring to my personal strengths. I can explain some targets for improvement.	I can explain how I contribute to teamwork, referring to my personal strengths. I can explain some targets for improvement. I can help others explain how their personal strengths can contribute to teamwork and help them explain targets for improvement.

This provides an opportunity to reflect on your Challenge topic as you progress through each skill.

Challenge topic review

Think about the challenge topic you have been exploring and complete the following statements.

I was surprised to discover that ....

I didn't know ....

I now think ....

Register to access free supporting resources through Cambridge GO – the home for all of your Cambridge digital content. Visit cambridge.org/go

Research

This section of your Learner's Skills Book 8 helps you to develop your research skills using interesting global topics.

Starting with . . .

As you start developing your research skills in Stage 8, you will be learning to explain to others what the term 'research' means and the steps you need to take towards conducting effective research using a search engine on the internet. You will recognise good and bad research questions, and begin to write your own relevant research questions. You will also be able to explain what certain texts are about and summarise the information gained from research in your own words.

Developing . . .

As you further develop your research skills in Stage 8, you will discuss different research methods for different purposes and how to write relevant questions to gain the information you need. You will design and give feedback on others' questionnaires to see if the questions asked help to answer the research questions posed. You will also continue to develop your ability to reference information sources accurately.

Getting better at . . .

As you get better at research during Stage 8, you will be exploring the uses of primary and secondary research methods for different purposes. You will also focus on how to record the information gained from both primary and secondary research. You will be analysing and creating graphs to present your findings after conducting primary research using a questionnaire. You will also be presenting an argument to convince others of a particular perspective.

1

Starting with research skills: Lesson 1

1.1 Construct relevant research questions

My learning goals are to start to:

- explain the term 'research'

- recognise a good research question

- write a good research question

How will I know if I reach my goals?

As you work through this lesson and achieve your learning goals, tick the 'Achieved' box to show you have completed this. If you haven't quite achieved your learning goals, tick 'Not there yet'. Start to think about how you are going to show your learning goals in your challenge. Add an example from your challenge once you have achieved each learning goal.

Lesson 1	Not there yet	Achieved	Example
I think I can explain the term 'research'.			
I can recognise a good research question.			
I can write at least one good research question.			

Prior learning

1 Which of these statements helps explain the term 'research'?
   Discuss this with a partner and write down your thoughts.

   A Copying information from the internet.

   B Studying information sources to find facts.

   C Asking people what they think about something.

   D Finding information to help answer a research question.

   ....

   ....

   ....

   ....

2 Do your classmates agree with you? Why?

   ....

3 Add one further idea to help explain what research is.

   ....

Starter activity

The topic I am working on today is …

....

1 Look at the research questions your teacher gives you.
   Which do you think are good research questions, and why?

   a Good research question: ....

      Why? ....

   b Good research question: ....

      Why? ....

2   Look at each research question again.
    Discuss it with your partner and answer the following questions:

    a   Is the question interesting?

    b   Is the question clear?

    c   Is the question too broad, too narrow or too vague?

    d   Is the question a leading question?

    e   Do you think you will be able to find information to help answer the question?

3   Do you still think that the questions you chose for task **1** are good research questions?
    Do your classmates agree?

    a   Yes/No
        Why?   ....

    b   Yes/No
        Why?   ....

Main activity

The topic I am working on today is …

....

1   Think of as many questions about the topic as you can, and write them on a mind map.

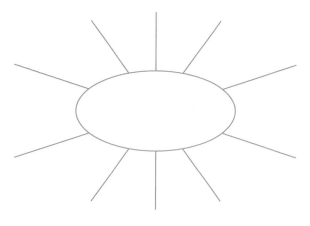

2 a Discuss your questions with a partner to check that the questions are relevant to the topic.

  b Now write three good research questions.
     Remember to check whether each of your questions:

- is interesting
- is clear
- is not leading
- is not too broad, too narrow or too vague
- can be answered after research.

     1 ....

     2 ....

     3 ....

  c Does your partner think that your questions are good research questions?

     1 Yes/No

       Why? ....

     2 Yes/No

       Why? ....

     3 Yes/No

       Why? ....

Class discussion

3 After class discussion on good and bad research questions, write down two more good research questions.

   1 ....

   2 ....

4 Reword your questions from task **2b** to make them even better research questions.

   1 ....

   2 ....

   3 ....

Independent reflection activity

What do you think has helped your learning in this lesson, and why?

A   Working on my own ....

B   Working with a partner ....

C   Whole-class discussion ....

D   Writing things down in my Learner's Skills Book ....

Which of these other skills do you think you have used today? Give an example.

A   Communication skills, as I listened to the ideas of others

B   Collaboration skills, as I worked with others and gave them some of my own ideas

C   Evaluation skills, as I explained what was good or bad about a research question

D   Reflection skills, as I thought about what helped me learn this lesson

....

....

....

....

Check your learning

If you haven't already done so, complete the **How will I know if I reach my goals?** table with 'Not there yet' or 'Achieved'. Don't forget to add examples from your challenge.

Starting with research skills: Lesson 2

1.3 Select an appropriate method and conduct research to test predictions and begin to answer a research question

1.4 Select, organise and record relevant information from a range of sources and findings from research, using appropriate methods

My learning goals are to start to:

- select appropriate research methods to begin to answer a research question
- summarise information from texts into my own words

How will I know if I reach my goals?

As you work through this lesson and achieve your learning goals, tick the 'Achieved' box to show you have completed this. If you haven't quite achieved your learning goals, tick 'Not there yet'. Start to think about how you are going to show your learning goals in your challenge. Add an example from your challenge once you have achieved each learning goal.

Lesson 2	Not there yet	Achieved	Example
I can select appropriate research methods.			
I can summarise information from a text in my own words.			

Prior learning

1   Which of these is the best research question, and why?

   A   Does urbanisation result in biodiversity and ecosystem loss?

   B   Why are more houses being built?

   C   What is responsible for the loss of wildlife?

   Best research question: ....

   ....

   Reason: ....

   ....

2   Do your classmates agree?   Yes/No

   Why? ....

   ....

Starter activity

1   What are the best ways of finding out information?
   Discuss with your partner and list as many ways as you can.

Ways of finding out information
1
2
3
4
5

Ways of finding out information
6
7
8
9
10

Class discussion

2 After a class discussion about ways of finding information, write down your top three ways of finding information to answer the best research question in the Prior learning activity. Explain your answers.

1 ....

because ....

2 ....

because ....

3 ....

because ....

Main activity

The topic I am working on today is …

....

1 Read the text your teacher gives you.

a Give the text a title.

b Discuss your title with a partner. Agree on the best title for the text.

Tip

To give a title to a text, you need to read the text to find out its main ideas. Look for words that are repeated throughout the text.

c Identify all the topic-specific words in the text and write them in the table.

Text title	
Topic	
Topic-specific words	

Peer feedback

d Share your topic-specific words with a partner.
Add to your ideas in a different colour.

e Share your text title and topic-specific words with classmates.
Agree on the best text title and add further topic-specific words to your table in a different colour.

2 Read each paragraph of the text again.

a Discuss each paragraph with a partner and give each one a sub-heading. Write the sub-headings in the table.

b Discuss the text with a partner. For each paragraph, summarise the information in your own words. Write two sentences for each paragraph.

> **Tip**
>
> Topic-specific words are words that are related to the text title.

> **Tip**
>
> To write a sub-heading, look for the key idea in the relevant paragraph.

Text title	
Main idea	Summary of each paragraph
Paragraph 1 sub-heading:	1 2

Paragraph 2 sub-heading:	1
	2
Paragraph 3 sub-heading:	1
	2

Tip

To summarise information given, you need to read it, think about it and write it in your own words.

Independent reflection activity

Which part of this lesson have you found interesting?
Choose one option below and explain why you found it interesting.

A   Giving the text a title

B   Sharing my ideas for the text title

C   Writing down topic-specific words

D   Giving each paragraph a sub-heading

E   Summarising each paragraph in my own words

Choice: ....

Reason: ....

Explain how you used evaluation skills today:

....

....

Check your learning

If you haven't already done so, complete the **How will I know if I reach my goals?** table with 'Not there yet' or 'Achieved'. Don't forget to add examples from your challenge.

3

Starting with research skills: Lesson 3

1.2 Identify and begin to reference a range of print and multimedia sources and use them to locate relevant information and answer research questions

1.3 Select an appropriate method and conduct research to test predictions and begin to answer a research question

1.4 Select, organise and record relevant information from a range of sources and findings from research, using appropriate methods

My learning goals are to start to:

- realise the importance of referencing information sources
- find relevant information about a topic
- reference sources of information accurately

How will I know if I reach my goals?

As you work through this lesson and achieve your learning goals, tick the 'Achieved' box to show you have completed this. If you haven't quite achieved your learning goals, tick 'Not there yet'. Start to think about how you are going to show your learning goals in your challenge. Add an example from your challenge once you have achieved each learning goal.

Lesson 3	Not there yet	Achieved	Example
I realise the importance of referencing information sources.			
I can find relevant information about a topic.			
I can reference a source of information with some accuracy.			

Prior learning

1 Why is it important to give credit to other people's work in your own work?

   A So that they receive money

   B Because it's respectful

   C So that you achieve the credit you deserve for your own work

   D Because you wouldn't like it if someone stole your ideas and passed them off as their own

   Explain your answer(s) ....

   ....

   Discuss your answer(s) with a partner. Do they agree? Write down their reasons.

   ....

2 Write down another reason why you think it's important to give credit to other people's work.

   ....

   ....

The topic I am working on today is …

....

Starter activity

1 Look at the reference your teacher shows you. Discuss the reference with your partner. Is it written correctly?   Yes/No

2 If it is not written correctly, what is missing?

   ....

3 Make up an example of a reference and write it correctly.

   ....

   ....

Tip

A reference list is a list of all the sources of information you have researched and used in your own work.

4   Share it with your teacher to check that it has all the necessary parts.
    Re-write the reference if it is missing any of the necessary parts.

    ....

    ....

Tip

To reference correctly, you need to include the author, the title of the article, the date it was published, the website address and the date you looked at the article.

Main activity

1   Using a search engine, find five newspaper articles containing
    information relevant to today's topic. Write down the website
    address for each article.

    A   ....

    B   ....

    C   ....

    D   ....

    E   ....

2   Discuss with a partner to check that each news article
    is relevant to today's topic.

3   Choose three of your news articles and write each reference
    correctly on the first line.

    Article 1: ....

    ....

    Article 2: ....

    ....

    Article 3: ....

    ....

Peer feedback

4   Check with your partner that you have written each reference correctly.
    If not, write out the references above again, in a different colour on the
    second line.

Independent reflection activity

Which part of today's lesson did you find the most challenging?

A   Explaining why it's important to give credit to someone else's work

B   Identifying what's missing from a reference

C   Writing a reference in the correct way

Choice: ....

Reason: ....

How have you used collaboration skills in today's lesson?

....

Check your learning

If you haven't already done so, complete the **How will I know if I reach my goals?** table with 'Not there yet' or 'Achieved'. Don't forget to add examples from your challenge.

Self-assessment 1

How much progress do you feel you have made so far in developing your research skills?

For each learning objective that follows, shade in the response that matches yours most closely. Give one example for this response. Eventually, you are aiming for green!

Learning objectives: to start to …	RED	AMBER	GREEN
1.1 Construct relevant research questions.	I know the features of a good research question, and can recognise good/bad research questions.	I know the features of a good research question, can recognise good and bad research questions and can write a good research question with help.	I know the features of a good research question, can recognise good and bad research questions and can write a good research question.

Continued			
Learning objectives: *to start to …*	RED	AMBER	GREEN
1.2 Identify and begin to reference a range of print and multimedia sources and use them to locate relevant information and answer research questions.	I understand why I need to give credit to someone else's work. I can reference at least one source of information with help, although this might not be completely accurate.	I understand why I need to add a reference list to my written work and can reference sources of information with some accuracy.	I understand the importance of reference lists and can reference at least one source of information accurately.
1.3 Select an appropriate method and conduct research to test predictions and begin to answer a research question.	I know some of the places I can get information from to start to answer a research question, and can use a search engine with help.	I know where to find relevant information to start to answer a research question, and can use a search engine.	I know how to use a search engine to gain relevant information to start to answer a research question, and can help others find relevant information.
1.4 Select, organise and record relevant information from a range of sources and findings from research, using appropriate methods.	I can state the main ideas contained within a text with help and can make notes in my own words to help summarise some of a text.	I can state the main ideas contained within a text and can use my own words to write some short sentences to summarise some of a text.	I can tell someone the main ideas contained within a text and use my own words to write a paragraph to summarise a short text.

Continued

Examples:

1.1 ....

1.2 ....

1.3 ....

1.4 ....

Reflect on your responses in your self-assessment and identify two areas for improvement. Set yourself two learning targets – how you will improve upon the two areas. For example: 'I will make sure that I add "(no date)" if there is no date for my reference.'

Learning targets:

1   Area for improvement: ....

    How I will improve: ....

2   Area for improvement: ....

    How I will improve: ....

Challenge topic review

Think about the challenge topic you have been exploring and complete the following statements.

I was surprised to discover that ....

I didn't know ....

I now think ....

4

Developing research skills: Lesson 4

1.1 Construct relevant research questions

How will I know if I reach my goals?

As you work through this lesson and achieve your learning goals, tick the 'Achieved' box to show you have completed this. If you haven't quite achieved your learning goals, tick 'Not there yet'. Start to think about how you are going to show your learning goals in your challenge. Add an example from your challenge once you have achieved each learning goal.

Lesson 4	Not there yet	Achieved	Example
I understand the features of a good research question.			
I can write a good research question.			
I can write sub-questions to help answer a research question.			

Prior learning

Discuss what a good research question is with your partner, then finish the sentence below with as many ideas as you can.

A good research question ...

....

....

....

Starter activity

1   Explain why these are bad research questions:

   a   What is biodiversity and ecosystem loss?

   ....

   b   Why are there so many homeless people in my town?

   ....

   c   Do you agree that tourism is good for a community?

   ....

   Do your classmates agree with you?   Yes/No

2   Work with your partner to make questions a–c in task 1 better research questions.

   a   ....

   b   ....

   c   ....

   Share with another pair. Do they have similar or better research questions?

Main activity

The topic I am working on today is …

....

Choose one of the sub-topics your teacher gives you.
In pairs, work through the following tasks.

1   What interests you about the topic?

   ....

2   Write three questions to do with the topic.

   1   ....

   2   ....

   3   ....

3   Look at your questions. What do they have in common?

   ....

   ....

4   Write down one possible research question.

   ....

   ....

5   Evaluate your question. (Is it interesting, clear and focused, and can it be argued?)

6   Reword your question.

   ....

   ....

7   Ask your teacher if your research question is a good question and suitable for the topic.

Tip

A good question is interesting, clear and focused, and can be argued.

Tip

A clear research question is a question that someone else can understand and would know what you are asking.

Tip

A focused research question is a question that is not too broad, too narrow or too vague. A question that is too broad makes it hard to find a clear answer. A question that is too narrow makes it hard to find enough information. A question that is too vague makes it difficult to know what to research.

8   Reword your question if needs be.

....

....

9   Now write down as many sub-questions as you can, to help you start
    your research to answer your research question.

    1   ....

    2   ....

    3   ....

    4   ....

    5   ....

    6   ....

    7   ....

    8   ....

Tip

A research question that can be argued allows you to develop or change your own personal perspective on the issue, supporting this personal perspective with evidence from research.

Independent reflection activity

Do you think this is a good research question?

How do young people become unemployed?   Yes/No

Why?...

....

Explain how you have used communication skills in today's lesson:

....

Check your learning

If you haven't already done so, complete the **How will I know if I reach my goals?** table
with 'Not there yet' or 'Achieved'. Don't forget to add examples from your challenge.

Developing research skills: Lesson 5

1.1 Construct relevant research questions

1.3 Select an appropriate method and conduct research to test predictions and begin to answer a research question

---

My learning goals are to develop my knowledge and understanding about:

- different research methods
- good questions for a questionnaire/survey
- writing questions to gain relevant information

How will I know if I reach my goals?

As you work through this lesson and achieve your learning goals, tick the 'Achieved' box on the following page to show you have completed this. If you haven't quite achieved your learning goals, tick 'Not there yet'. Start to think about how you are going to show your learning goals in your challenge. Add an example from your challenge once you have achieved each learning goal.

How will I know if I reach my goals?

Lesson 5	Not there yet	Achieved	Example
I can explain the difference between research methods.			
I can identify good questions to put in a questionnaire.			
I can write good questions to gain relevant information.			

Prior learning

When you want to develop a local perspective about an issue, which research method(s) do you choose? Discuss this with a partner and explain your choice(s).

A   Questionnaire   C   Internet   E   Other …

B   Interview   D   Newspaper

....

....

....

Starter activity

1   Number these five options (**A–E**) in order, with **1** as the most important when writing questions for a questionnaire.

Questions to gain information should:

A   use words that have clear meanings   ....

B   be short   ....

C   be able to be answered quickly   ....

D   not offer too many options   ....

E   not be leading or contain bias.   ....

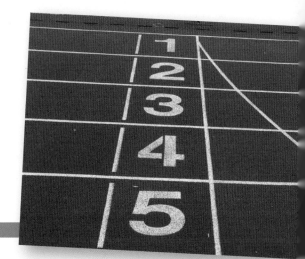

2   After a class discussion about questions for questionnaires to gain information, did you change your mind about the order of the options in task **1**?   Yes/No

Why? ....

....

Main activity

The topic I am working on today is …

....

Look at the questionnaire your teacher gives you. Discuss it with a partner and answer the following questions.

1   Is this a good questionnaire?   Yes/No

Why? ....

....

....

> **Tip**
>
> Good questions should not be leading.

> **Tip**
>
> Good questions should not contain bias. 'Why don't more people use public transport and leave their cars at home?' is an example of a biased question.

> **Tip**
>
> Good questions should be clearly worded.

> **Tip**
>
> Good questions should not give too many options.

2 Answer the questions on the questionnaire.
Which ones did you find difficult to answer? Why?

....

....

....

Tip

Some questions
will require a 'yes'
or 'no' answer.
Others will ask for
more detail.

Class discussion

3 As a class, discuss the features of good and bad questions.

4 Do you still think this is a good questionnaire?   Yes/No

Why? ....

....

5 Using what you have learnt from class discussion, write five
questions to gain relevant information about today's topic.

1	
2	
3	
4	
5	

6 Share your questions with a partner.
Do they think your questions are good?   Yes/No

Why? ....

....

Independent reflection activity

What helped you learn today?

....

....

How did you develop your reflection skills in today's lesson?

....

....

Check your learning

If you haven't already done so, complete the **How will I know if I reach my goals?** table with 'Not there yet' or 'Achieved'. Don't forget to add examples from your challenge.

6

Developing research skills: Lesson 6

1.2 Identify and begin to reference a range of print and multimedia sources and use them to locate relevant information and answer research questions

1.3 Select an appropriate method and conduct research to test predictions and begin to answer a research question

1.4 Select, organise and record relevant information from a range of sources and findings from research, using appropriate methods

My learning goals are to develop my knowledge and understanding about:

- recognising good questions to test predictions
- writing questionnaires to gain relevant information
- selecting information to write questions
- referencing sources of information

How will I know if I reach my goals?

As you work through this lesson and achieve your learning goals, tick the 'Achieved' box to show you have completed this. If you haven't quite achieved your learning goals, tick 'Not there yet'. Start to think about how you are going to show your learning goals in your challenge. Add an example from your challenge once you have achieved each learning goal.

Lesson 6	Not there yet	Achieved	Example
I can recognise good questions to test predictions.			
I can write questions to gain relevant information.			
I can select relevant information to write questions.			
I can reference the sources of information I use to write questions.			

Prior learning

1   Which of these are good questions to find out whether cars are the main source of air pollution in a city? Discuss these questions with a partner before recording your responses in task **2**.

   A   Do you agree that air pollution is a problem in our city?

   Yes ☐

   B   What do you think is the main cause of air pollution in our city?

   Industry ☐   Cars ☐

   Other ....

   C   Do you think air pollution is harmful to animals?

   Yes ☐   No ☐   Maybe ☐

   D   Do you think air pollution would decrease if there were fewer cars in our city?

   Yes ☐   No ☐

   Why? ....

Continued

2 What do you think about the questions in task **1**?

A I think question .... is a good question because

....

B I think question .... is a good question because

....

3 Do your classmates agree with you? Why, or why not?

....

....

Tip

A prediction is a statement about what you think will happen or what you think is causing something to happen; for example, 'Increased traffic will increase levels of air pollution', or 'People living in poverty suffer from poor health'.

The topic I am working on today is …

....

Starter activity

1 Work on one of the statements your teacher shows you. Discuss it with a partner and write down some questions to find information related to the statement.

When ....?

What ....?

Which ....?

Who ....?

Where ....?

Why ....?

How ....?

2 Share your questions with your classmates.
Which question do you think is the best? Why?

Question ....

Reason ....

Tip

To test a
prediction, the
right type of
question needs
to be asked.

Main activity

1 Using a separate piece of paper and appropriate sources, write a
questionnaire to gain information related to your topic.

2 Write out the reference for each of the sources of information
you used to write your questions.

....

....

....

....

....

....

....

....

....

Tip

Primary research
enables the
researcher to
gain a first-hand
account of events
or opinions about
issues.

Tip

A primary
research source
is usually gained
by talking with
someone or
asking them to
complete a survey
or questionnaire
about a topic.

3 Read and evaluate another pair's questionnaire.
Ask the following questions.

A Are there any leading questions?   Yes/No

B Do any of the questions contain bias?   Yes/No

C Are all the questions clearly worded?   Yes/No

D Are there too many/too few options for any of the questions? Yes/No

E Is there a balance between questions requiring 'yes/no' answers and those needing more detail? Yes/No

4 Before the next lesson, give your questionnaire to ten people to complete. Collect the completed questionnaires and bring them to the lesson.

Independent reflection activity

What did you find challenging about today's lesson?

....

....

How did you overcome this challenge?

....

....

What other skills have you used today? Give examples.

....

....

Check your learning

If you haven't already done so, complete the **How will I know if I reach my goals?** table with 'Not there yet' or 'Achieved'. Don't forget to add examples from your challenge.

Self-assessment 2

Look back at Self-assessment 1. How much further progress do you feel you have made in developing your research skills?

For each learning objective below, shade in the response that matches yours most closely. Give one example for this response. Eventually, you are aiming for green!

Learning objectives: *to develop my knowledge and understanding about how to ...*	RED	AMBER	GREEN
1.1 Construct relevant research questions.	I know the features of a good research question and can write a good research question with help.	I know the features of a good research question and can write good research questions.	I know the features of a good research question, can write good research questions and can help others write good research questions.
1.2 Identify and begin to reference a range of print and multimedia sources and use them to locate relevant information and answer research questions.	I understand the importance of reference lists and can reference some sources of information with some accuracy.	I understand the importance of reference lists and can reference at least one source of information accurately.	I understand the importance of reference lists, can reference at least one source of information accurately and can help others with referencing.

Continued

Learning objectives: *to develop my knowledge and understanding about how to ...*	RED	AMBER	GREEN
1.3 Select an appropriate method and conduct research to test predictions and begin to answer a research question.	I know one of the research methods to use when starting to develop a local perspective on a topic/issue and can write a question to test a prediction with help.	I know which research methods to use to develop a local perspective on a topic/issue and can write a question to test a prediction.	I know which research methods to use to develop a local perspective on a topic/issue and can write questions to test more than one prediction. I can help others write questions to test predictions.
1.4 Select, organise and record relevant information from a range of sources and findings from research, using appropriate methods.	I can record some relevant information from an information source in my own words with help.	I can record some relevant information from an information source in my own words.	I can record relevant information from an information source in my own words and can help others record relevant information.

Examples:

1.1 ....

1.2 ....

1.3 ....

1.4 ....

Continued

Reflect on your responses in your self-assessment and identify two areas for improvement. Set yourself two learning targets – how you will improve upon the two areas. For example: 'I will help someone in class to write a good research question.'

Learning targets:

1 Area for improvement: ....

   How I will improve: ....

2 Area for improvement: ....

   How I will improve: ....

Challenge topic review

Think about the challenge topic you have been exploring and complete the following statements.

I was surprised to discover that ....

I didn't know ....

I now think ....

7

Getting better at research skills: Lesson 7

1.3 Select an appropriate method and conduct research to test predictions and begin to answer a research question

1.4 Select, organise and record relevant information from a range of sources and findings from research, using appropriate methods

My learning goals are to get better at:

- understanding how research helps test a prediction
- recording information gained from primary research
- presenting information gained from primary research

How will I know if I reach my goals?

As you work through this lesson and achieve your learning goals, tick the 'Achieved' box to show you have completed this. If you haven't quite achieved your learning goals, tick 'Not there yet'. Start to think about how you are going to show your learning goals in your challenge. Add an example from your challenge once you have achieved each learning goal.

Lesson 7	Not there yet	Achieved	Example
I understand how research helps test a prediction.			
I can select and record relevant information.			
I can present information gained from primary research in an appropriate way.			

Prior learning

1   Discuss predictions with your partner and then finish these sentences.

   a   A prediction is ....

   ....

   b   To test a prediction, you need to ....

   ....

   Share your ideas in class.

2   Using what you have learnt, summarise in your own words how research helps test a prediction.

   ....

   ....

Starter activity

1   Study the source of information your teacher gives you. Discuss it with your partner and then answer the following questions.

   a   What kind of information source is it?

   ....

   b   Who created the source? What do you know about them?

   ....

   c   When was the source created?

   ....

   d   Why do you think the source was created?

   ....

e Who do you think is the audience for the source?

....

f Do you think the source is clear?   Yes/No

Why? ....

Class discussion

2 Using your learning from class discussion, add to or change any of your answers in task **1** with a different coloured pen.

Main activity

The topic I am working on today is …

....

1 Discuss and decide with your partner how you might present your research findings from your questionnaire in Lesson 6.

- ....

- ....

- ....

- ....

2 Do your classmates agree?   Yes/No

Why? ....

....

3 Choose a way of presenting your findings and check with your teacher if this is suitable.

....

> **Tip**
>
> You need to find the most appropriate way of presenting your research findings, according to the purpose of your research and your audience.

> **Tip**
>
> Try to present your research findings as clearly as you can. Include headings and clear titles.

4   Summarise in your own words your research findings from Lesson 6.

....

....

....

....

....

....

....

Independent reflection activity

What has helped you learn today?

....

....

How have you helped someone else learn today?

....

....

....

....

Check your learning

If you haven't already done so, complete the **How will I know if I reach my goals?** table with 'Not there yet' or 'Achieved'. Don't forget to add examples from your challenge.

Getting better at research skills: Lesson 8

1.1 Construct relevant research questions

1.3 Select an appropriate method and conduct research to test predictions and begin to answer a research question

1.4 Select, organise and record relevant information from a range of sources and findings from research, using appropriate methods

My learning goals are to get better at:

- understanding when to use primary and secondary information sources
- doing an internet search to find relevant information
- judging the quality of an information source to help answer a research question

How will I know if I reach my goals?

As you work through this lesson and achieve your learning goals, tick the 'Achieved' box to show you have completed this. If you haven't quite achieved your learning goals, tick 'Not there yet'. Start to think about how you are going to show your learning goals in your challenge. Add an example from your challenge once you have achieved each learning goal.

Lesson 8	Not there yet	Achieved	Example
I understand when to use primary and secondary sources of information.			
I know how to do an internet search to find relevant information.			
I can judge the quality of an information source to help answer a research question.			

Prior learning

1   Discuss with your partner examples of primary and secondary sources of information.

   a   Primary ....

   ....

   b   Secondary ....

   ....

2   Using what you have learnt from class discussion, answer this question.

   When might you need to use primary and secondary sources of information?

   a   Primary ....

   ....

   b   Secondary ....

   ....

Starter activity

Describe the missing steps for researching information on the internet.

1   Decide what information you need to find. ....

2   ....

3   ....

4   ....

5   ....

> **Tip**
>
> If the name of a website ends with '.gov' and then a country abbreviation (e.g. '.uk' or '.my'), it is probably a reliable government website.

Main activity

The topic I am working on today is …

....

Look at the text your teacher gives you.

1   Discuss the source with a partner and answer the following questions.

    a   What is the title of the source?

      ....

    b   Who is the author?

      ....

    c   When was the source written?

      ....

    d   What is the topic and the main idea?

      ....

      ....

    e   What do you think the author's opinion about the topic is?

      ....

      ....

    f   What evidence is there to support the author's opinion?

      ....

      ....

Tip

If the website ends in '.org', it is probably the website of a non-profit organisation. These websites are good information sources but are probably biased.

Tip

If the website address contains 'wiki', be careful, as wiki and social media websites can be edited by anyone so the information might not be true. Always cross-reference information obtained from this type of website.

g   Overall, do you think the author's argument is convincing? Why, or why not?

....

....

h   How reliable do you think the source is?

....

....

i   Write a research question that this source of information will help to answer.

....

....

> **Tip**
>
> A reliable source is one that lacks bias, is kept updated, is complete and error-free, and the author and publication can be checked.

Class discussion

2   Using what you have learnt from class discussion, add to or change any of your answers for task **1** with a different coloured pen.

> **Independent reflection activity**
>
> What have you found challenging today?
>
> ....
>
> How have you addressed this challenge?
>
> ....
>
> How have you used communication skills today?
>
> ....

> **Check your learning**
>
> If you haven't already done so, complete the **How will I know if I reach my goals?** table with 'Not there yet' or 'Achieved'. Don't forget to add examples from your challenge.

Getting better at research skills: Lesson 9

1.2 Identify and begin to reference a range of print and multimedia sources and use them to locate relevant information and answer research questions

1.3 Select an appropriate method and conduct research to test predictions and begin to answer a research question

1.4 Select, organise and record relevant information from a range of sources and findings from research, using appropriate methods

My learning goals are to get better at:

- referencing sources of information
- finding relevant information to answer a research question
- recording relevant information

How will I know if I reach my goals?

As you work through this lesson and achieve your learning goals, tick the 'Achieved' box to show you have completed this. If you haven't quite achieved your learning goals, tick 'Not there yet'. Start to think about how you are going to show your learning goals in your challenge. Add an example from your challenge once you have achieved each learning goal.

Lesson 9	Not there yet	Achieved	Example
I can reference some sources of information accurately.			
I can find some relevant information using a search engine.			
I can record some relevant information in my own words.			

Prior learning

Why is a search engine useful? Discuss this with a partner.

A search engine is useful because ....

....

To use a search engine you need to ....

....

The topic I am working on today is …

....

Starter activity

Look at the picture your teacher has given you.

1   Discuss the picture with a partner. What words/phrases, issue(s) and perspective(s) come to mind when looking at it?

Words: ....

....

Phrases: ....

....

Issue(s): ....

....

Perspective(s): ....

....

Class discussion

2   After a class discussion, add to your lists in task **1** in a different colour.

Main activity

1   Work in teams of four with your picture from the Starter Activity. Look at the website addresses your teacher has given you, then find a fourth website that is relevant to your issue.

2   Each team member chooses one website to use for research. Write down the website you are using to gain information.

....

3   Give the full reference of the article you are using.

....

....

> **Tip**
>
> You need to be clear about your reason for looking for information.

4   Write notes on what you have learnt about the topic from your website.

....

....

....

....

....

....

5   Share the information you have gained with your team.

6   In your team, decide on the best presentation method for your perspective. Explain why.

Method: ....

Why: ....

....

Independent reflection activity

Explain the most important thing that helped you learn today.

....

....

List the skills you have used today. Explain how you used these skills.

....

....

Check your learning

If you haven't already done so, complete the **How will I know if I reach my goals?** table with 'Not there yet' or 'Achieved'. Don't forget to add examples from your challenge.

Self-assessment 3

Look back at Self-assessments 1 and 2. How much further progress do you feel you have made in developing your research skills?

For each learning objective below, shade in the response that matches yours most closely. Give one example for this response. Eventually, you are aiming for green!

Learning objectives: *to get better at understanding how to ...*	RED	AMBER	GREEN
1.1 Construct relevant research questions.	I know some of the features of a good research question and can write a good, relevant research question with help.	I know the features of a good research question and can write a good, relevant research question.	I can write a good research question and can help others write good, relevant research questions.
1.2 Identify and begin to reference a range of print and multimedia sources and use them to locate relevant information and answer research questions.	I know the importance of reference lists and can reference at least one source of information with some accuracy. I can use a reference to find some relevant information for a specific purpose with help.	I know the importance of reference lists and can reference at least one source of information accurately. I can use a reference to find some relevant information for a specific purpose.	I know the importance of reference lists and can reference sources of information accurately. I can use a reference to find relevant information and help others find relevant information for a specific purpose.

Continued

Learning objectives: *to get better at understanding how to ...*	RED	AMBER	GREEN
1.3 Select an appropriate method and conduct research to test predictions and begin to answer a research question.	I know what a prediction is and have some understanding of how research can help test a prediction. I can do an internet search to find some relevant information with help.	I know what a prediction is and understand how research can help test a prediction. I can do an internet search to find some relevant information.	I understand what a prediction is and can explain this to others. I understand how research can help test a prediction. I can do an internet search to find some relevant information and can show others how to do an internet search.
1.4 Select, organise and record relevant information from a range of sources and findings from research, using appropriate methods.	I can select and record relevant information from at least one information source with help. I can present some of this information in some of my own words in a suitable way.	I can select and record relevant information from more than one information source. I can present relevant information from these sources in my own words in a suitable way.	I can select and record relevant information from some different information sources. I can present relevant information from these sources in my own words in a suitable way and I can help others select, organise and record relevant information.

Continued

Examples:

1.1 ....

1.2 ....

1.3 ....

1.4 ....

Reflect on your responses in your self-assessment and identify two areas for improvement. Set yourself two learning targets – how you will improve upon the two areas. For example: 'I will show others how to select, organise and record relevant information from an information source'.

Learning targets:

1   Area for improvement: ....

    How I will improve: ....

2   Area for improvement: ....

    How I will improve: ....

Challenge topic review

Think about the challenge topic you have been exploring and complete the following statements.

I was surprised to discover that ....

I didn't know ....

I now think ....

Analysis

This section of your Learner's Skills Book 8 helps you to develop your analysis skills using interesting global topics.

Starting with . . .

As you start to develop your analysis skills in Stage 8, you will be learning how to explain the term 'analysis' and how to analyse something. You will summarise relevant information gained from discussion with classmates. You will learn the difference between an issue, a perspective and a course of action, and be able to explain these and give relevant examples. You will also learn how to analyse data to help support an argument and create your own bar graph to present research findings.

Developing . . .

As you further develop your analysis skills in Stage 8, you will discuss the type of questions you might ask before being able to resolve an issue and how you might take action to help resolve or make a positive difference to an issue. You will focus on understanding the difference between a global, a national, a local and a personal perspective. You will be able to give examples for these perspectives and explore how the evidence gained from graphs can be used to support an argument and explain the causes and consequences of issues.

Getting better at . . .

As you get better at analysing topics and issues in Stage 8, you will be focusing on understanding key Global Perspectives terms, identifying different groups of stakeholders and explaining the perspective of a specific group of stakeholders. You will focus on gaining information from different perspectives by analysing texts and designing questionnaires. You will then analyse the data gained from your questionnaire and use your research findings to suggest a course of action and produce an outcome to help resolve or make a positive difference to an issue.

Starting with analysis skills: Lesson 1

2.1 Identify ideas and evidence from different perspectives within different sources on a given topic

2.3 Explain causes of a local or global issue and consequences on others

---

My learning goals are to start to:

- explain the term 'analysis'
- explain how to analyse something
- summarise relevant information

How will I know if I reach my goals?

As you work through this lesson and you achieve your learning goals, tick the 'Achieved' box to show you have completed this. If you haven't quite achieved your learning goals, tick 'Not there yet'. Start to think about how you are going to show your learning goals in your challenge. Add an example from your challenge once you have achieved each learning goal.

Lesson 1	Not there yet	Achieved	Example
I can explain the term 'analysis'.			
I can explain how to analyse something.			
I can summarise relevant information.			

Prior learning

1 Look at the picture your teacher shows you. Discuss it with a partner. Write down as many words and phrases as you can about the picture in the time your teacher gives you.

....

....

2 Discuss the picture and your words and phrases with another pair.
   Add further words and phrases to your list.

The topic I am working on today is ...

....

Starter activity

1 Using your list of words and phrases from your prior learning, work with your partner to explain what you think the picture shows.

   The picture shows ....

   ....

   ....

2 What do you think the term 'analysis' means?

   ....

Peer feedback

3 Does your partner agree?   Yes/No

Main activity

1 Choose one of the sub-topics your teacher gives you for discussion with your group. As a group, answer the following questions:

a What is the sub-topic about?

....

b Why do you think the sub-topic might be of national/local importance?

....

c Why do you think the sub-topic might be a global issue?

....

d What are your group's views about the sub-topic?

....

e Why did you choose this sub-topic?

....

2 As a result of your discussion, write a commentary for your sub-topic. Then record your commentary.

....

....

....

....

....

....

> **Tip**
>
> When analysing a topic or sub-topic, break it down into the important parts that make it up. You need to explain the topic or sub-topic in more detail.

> **Tip**
>
> Analysis can focus on the causes of or reasons for a situation or issue. It can show the consequences of a situation or issue. For example, gaining weight can be a consequence of eating too much fatty food.

> **Tip**
>
> Analysis can also be perspectives, viewpoints or reactions to a situation or issue.

3   Listen to some of the commentaries and write notes to record the information gained.

	Sub-topic	Information gained
1		
2		
3		

4   What type of information have you gained?

....

....

5   Reflecting on what you have learnt, what do you need to do to analyse something?

....

Independent reflection activity

Which part of today's lesson did you find the most difficult?

....

Why do you think this was?

....

What skills have you used today?

....

Check your learning

If you haven't already done so, complete the **How will I know if I reach my goals?** table with 'Not there yet' or 'Achieved'. Don't forget to add examples from your challenge.

Starting with analysis skills: Lesson 2

2.1 Identify ideas and evidence from different perspectives within different sources on a given topic

Prior learning

1   Discuss with a partner and then write down any words and/or phrases that signal a cause or reason for something happening.

   ....

2   Discuss with your partner and then write down any words and/or phrases that signal a consequence or result of something happening.

   ....

   ....

3   Do you have the same words and/or phrases as your classmates? Add to your list in a different colour.

The topic I am working on today is ...

....

Starter activity

1   Look at the sub-topic your teacher shows you. Discuss it with a partner. How many issues to do with this sub-topic can you come up with?

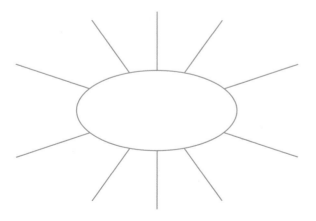

Tip

An issue is an important topic/sub-topic or problem for debate or discussion.

Tip

An issue often needs a solution. For example, the issue of increased greenhouse gas emissions might be resolved by planting more trees.

Peer feedback

2   Share your mind map with another pair. Have they identified issues you had not thought of? Yes/No

Further issues: ....

3   Using what you've learnt from your discussion about issues, in your own words explain what an issue is.

An issue is ....

4   How do you think an issue differs from a perspective?

....

5   Does your partner agree?   Yes/No

6   Check with your teacher that you know the difference between an issue and a perspective.

Main activity

1   Using the text your teacher gives you, answer the following questions.

a   What is/are the issue(s)?

....

....

b   What is/are the perspective(s)?

....

....

c   What other information is included in the text?

....

....

Tip

A perspective is a certain world view or way of looking at an issue.

Tip

A personal perspective is the view that a person has on an issue after exploring different perspectives and reflecting on the causes and consequences of an issue.

Tip

A national perspective is the view that a particular country has on an issue. This is usually explained by the laws, policies and/or speeches made by politicians of that country and might be supported by other groups within that country.

Class discussion

2   Using what you have learnt from class discussion about issues and perspectives, give three further examples of issues and perspectives for the topic/sub-topic you are working on.

	Issue	Perspective
1		
2		
3		

3   Share your three issues and perspectives with your partner.

4   Do you think your partner understands the difference between an issue and a perspective? Why do you think so?   Yes/No

   Reason: ....

Independent reflection activity

Which part of this lesson did you find interesting? Why?

A Explaining an issue ....

B Explaining a global perspective ....

C Explaining a national perspective ....

D Other ....

How have you used research skills today?

....

....

Check your learning

If you haven't already done so, complete the **How will I know if I reach my goals?** table with 'Not there yet' or 'Achieved'. Don't forget to add examples from your challenge.

3

Starting with analysis skills: Lesson 3

2.1 Identify ideas and evidence from different perspectives within different sources on a given topic

2.2 Explain how graphical or numerical data supports an argument

2.4 Suggest and justify different actions to make a positive difference to a national or global issue

My learning goals are to start to:

- understand the difference between an issue, a perspective and a course of action
- explain how data from a graph can support an argument
- suggest courses of action to make a positive difference to an issue

How will I know if I reach my goals?

As you work through this lesson and you achieve your learning goals, tick the 'Achieved' box to show you have completed this. If you haven't quite achieved your learning goals, tick 'Not there yet'. Start to think about how you are going to show your learning goals in your challenge. Add an example from your challenge once you have achieved each learning goal.

Lesson 3	Not there yet	Achieved	Example
I think I know the difference between an issue, a perspective and a course of action.			
I can explain how data from a graph can support an argument.			
I can suggest a course of action to make a positive difference to an issue.			

Prior learning

1   Use your prior knowledge and any new learning about issues, perspectives and courses of action, to explain the following terms to your partner.

   a   An issue is ....

   b   A perspective is ....

   c   A course of action is ....

2   Is your own understanding about the difference between issues, perspectives and courses of action now clearer?   Yes/No

   Why? ....

3   Give an example for each of the following:

   a   an issue ....

   b   a perspective ....

   c   a course of action ....

The topic I am working on today is …

....

Starter activity

1   Look at the graph your teacher shows you. Discuss it with a partner.
2   Write down and answer the questions your teacher gives you.

   a   ....

      ....

   b   ....

      ....

c ....

....

d ....

....

e ....

....

f ....

....

3 What argument do you think the information gained from this graph might help support?

....

....

....

> **Tip**
>
> A course of action is something you can do to help make a positive difference to an issue.

Main activity

1 Look at the data your teacher gives you. Discuss it with your partner. Make some predictions based on the data.

a We predict ....

....

b We predict ....

....

c We predict ....

....

> **Tip**
>
> A bar graph can help you present your research findings, but you should also add some text to explain what your bar graph shows.

2 Create a double bar graph using the data.

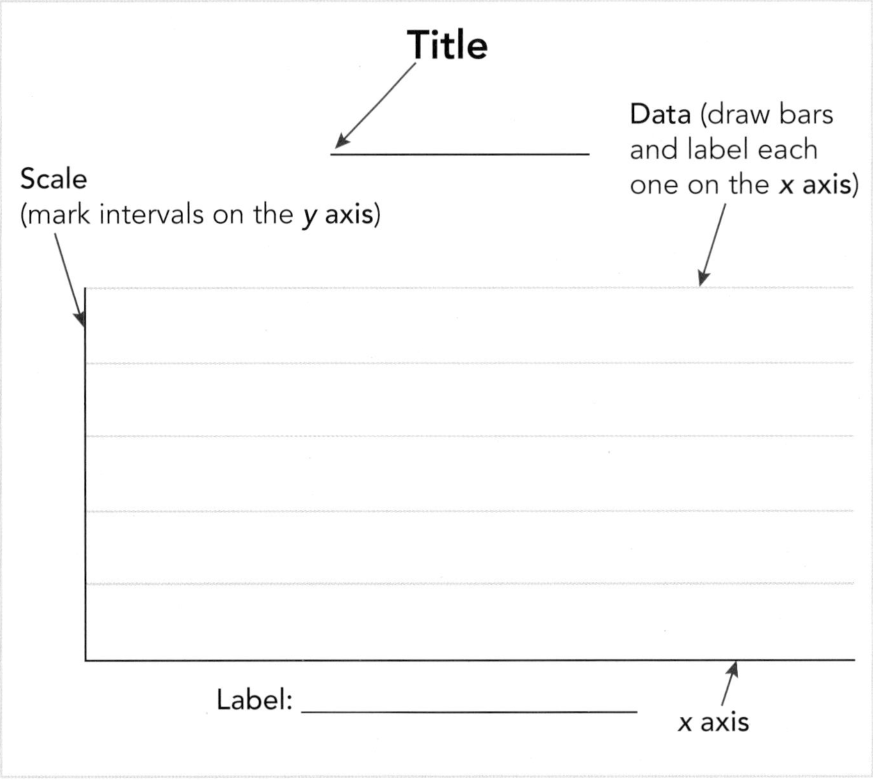

Title

Data (draw bars and label each one on the **x axis**)

Scale
(mark intervals on the **y axis**)

Label: _____

x axis

Tip

You can use a bar graph as evidence to support a particular argument you make. For example, the graph shows that family upbringing is a key factor for people choosing the foods they eat.

3 Check your predictions against your graph. Answer the following questions.

a How does the data compare with your predictions?

....

b Which of your predictions were close to the actual data?

....

Tip

A double bar graph allows for comparison; for example, between male and female or between two different countries.

c Which of your predictions were not close to the actual data?

....

4 What action(s) might you take to influence people in a positive way about the topic/sub-topic you have learnt about in this lesson?

....

....

Tip

A prediction is a statement about what you think might happen or what you think might cause something to happen.

Class discussion

5   Discuss your graph with your classmates. Do the graphs look
     similar? If not, discuss where the differences are and why there
     might be differences.

Independent reflection activity

What have you learnt today?

....

What has helped you to learn today?

....

What skills have you used today?

....

Check your learning

If you haven't already done so, complete the **How will I know if I reach my goals?** table
with 'Not there yet' or 'Achieved'. Don't forget to add examples from your challenge.

Self-assessment 1

How much progress do you feel you have made so far in developing your analysis skills?

For each learning objective in the table, shade in the response that matches yours most closely. Give one example for this response. Eventually, you are aiming for green!

Learning objectives: *to start to …*	RED	AMBER	GREEN
2.1 Identify ideas and evidence from different perspectives within different sources on a given topic.	I can identify ideas and evidence from different perspectives with help. I can summarise relevant information with help.	I can identify ideas and evidence from different perspectives. I can summarise relevant information.	I can identify ideas and evidence from different perspectives. I can summarise relevant information. I can help others identify ideas and evidence from different perspectives and help them summarise relevant information.
2.2 Explain how graphical or numerical data supports an argument.	I know why graphs are used. I can identify information from a graph with help. I can create a graph with help.	I understand the importance of graphs as evidence to help support an argument. I can identify relevant information from a graph. I can create a graph to show research findings.	I understand the importance of graphs as evidence to help support an argument. I can identify relevant information from graph. I can create a graph to show research findings and I can help others create graphs.

Continued

Learning objectives: *to start to ...*	RED	AMBER	GREEN
2.3 Explain causes of a local or global issue and consequences on others.	I know what the term 'analysis' means. I can explain how to analyse something with help. I can recognise causes and consequences of an issue with help.	I know what the term 'analysis' means. I can explain how to analyse something. I can recognise causes and consequences of an issue.	I know what the term 'analysis' means. I can explain how to analyse something. I can recognise causes and consequences of an issue and help others recognise the causes and consequences of an issue.
2.4 Suggest and justify different actions to make a positive difference to a national or global issue.	I can explain the difference between an issue, a perspective and a course of action with help. I can suggest an action to make a positive difference to an issue with help.	I can explain the difference between an issue, a perspective and a course of action and give an example for each. I can suggest relevant actions to make a positive difference to an issue.	I can explain the difference between an issue, a perspective and a course of action and give examples for each. I can suggest relevant actions to make a positive difference to an issue and help others propose relevant actions to make a positive difference to an issue.

Examples:

2.1 ....

2.2 ....

2.3 ....

2.4 ....

Continued

Reflect on your responses in your self-assessment and identify two areas for improvement. Set yourself two learning targets – how you will improve upon the two areas. For example, 'I will try to help others understand the difference between a global and national perspective.

Learning targets:

1 Area for improvement: ....

   How I will improve: ....

2 Area for improvement: ....

   How I will improve: ....

Challenge topic review

Think about the challenge topic you have been exploring and complete the statements.

I was surprised to discover that ....

I didn't know ....

I now think ....

4

Developing analysis skills: Lesson 4

2.4 Suggest and justify different actions to make a positive difference to a national or global issue

How will I know if I reach my goals?

As you work through this lesson and you achieve your learning goals, tick the 'Achieved' box to show you have completed this. If you haven't quite achieved your learning goals, tick 'Not there yet'. Start to think about how you are going to show your learning goals in your challenge. Add an example from your challenge once you have achieved each learning goal.

Lesson 4	Not there yet	Achieved	Example
I know some questions to ask to decide on a suitable course of action to help resolve an issue.			
I can suggest different actions to help resolve or make a positive difference to an issue.			

Prior learning

1   Work with a partner or in a small group. Read the text your teacher gives you.
    What are the issues?

    1   ....

    2   ....

    3   ....

    4   ....

    5   ....

2   Do your classmates agree with you?
    Make any changes to your list of issues in a different colour.

Starter activity

1   What questions might you ask before attempting to solve
    a problem?

    a   What .... ?

    b   Why .... ?

    c   Who .... ?

    d   Which .... ?

    e   Where .... ?

    f   How .... ?

Tip

Courses of action need to be realistic, e.g. giving a presentation to help raise awareness to make a positive difference to an issue.

2   Do your classmates have different questions?
Write down the best three questions.

1   ....

2   ....

3   ....

The topic I am working on today is …

....

Main activity

1   Choose one of the issues your teacher has given you and complete the following table.

Issue (as a question)		
Possible action	Reasons for/against	Other factors
1		
2		
3		

Class discussion

2 Using what you've learnt from partner and class discussion about courses and action, decide on your best possible course of action to help resolve your chosen issue and give reasons for your choice.

Course of action: ....

....

Reasons for this choice: ....

....

Tip

There may be many different actions that can help make a positive difference to an issue. Choose one most suitable for the issue.

Independent reflection activity

Do you think it might now be easier for you to come up with different types of action to help resolve issues?

....

Why? ....

....

As well as analysis skills, which other skills have you used today?

....

Check your learning

If you haven't already done so, complete the **How will I know if I reach my goals?** table with 'Not there yet' or 'Achieved'. Don't forget to add examples from your challenge.

Developing analysis skills: Lesson 5

2.1 Identify ideas and evidence from different perspectives within different sources on a given topic

2.2 Explain how graphical or numerical data supports an argument

2.3 Explain causes of a local or global issue and consequences on others

My learning goals are to develop my knowledge and understanding about:

- the difference between a local and a personal perspective

- how graphs can be used as evidence to support an argument

- how to explain the causes and consequences of issues

How will I know if I reach my goals?

As you work through this lesson and you achieve your learning goals, tick the 'Achieved' box to show you have completed this. If you haven't quite achieved your learning goals, tick 'Not there yet'. Start to think about how you are going to show your learning goals in your challenge. Add an example from your challenge once you have achieved each learning goal.

Lesson 5	Not there yet	Achieved	Example
I understand the difference between a local and a personal perspective.			
I can recognise how a graph can be used as evidence to support an argument.			
I can explain some causes and consequences of an issue.			

Prior learning

1   Discuss with a partner. What do you think each of these terms means?

   a   A local perspective: ....

   ....

   b   A personal perspective: ....

   ....

2   Discuss your ideas with your classmates. Do they agree? Yes/No

3   Do you now understand the difference between a local and personal perspective better?   Yes/No

   Give an example for each.

   a   A local perspective: ....

   ....

   b   A personal perspective: ....

   ....

> **Tip**
>
> Different communities can have different or similar local perspectives depending on the topic or issue. A local perspective is not simply information about a community or what a community is doing, it is the view that a particular community has about an issue.

The topic I am working on today is …

....

Starter activity

Look at the graph your teacher shows you.

1   What does the graph show?

   ....

2   What argument might the evidence in the graph help support?

   ....

   ....

3   What do you find interesting about the evidence in the graph?

    ....

4   Do your classmates agree?   Yes/No

Main activity

1   Look at the text your teacher gives you and discuss it with a partner.

2   Answer the following questions:

    a   What is the main idea of the text?

        ....

        ....

    b   Write down some topic-specific words and phrases.

        ....

        ....

    c   Are specific issues mentioned? If so, what are they?

        ....

        ....

    d   Are any causes of the specific issues mentioned? If so, what are they?

        ....

        ....

        ....

    e   Are any consequences mentioned? If so, what are they?

        ....

        ....

        ....

> **Tip**
>
> A local perspective is usually explained by local policies and speeches made by local politicians of a country and might be supported by other groups within that community, such as religious groups.

> **Tip**
>
> A personal perspective is what you think about a topic/ issue as a result of any research findings.

> **Tip**
>
> Your personal perspective can develop or change as you become more informed about a topic or issue.

f What different perspectives are given?

....

....

....

g What course(s) of action are referred to?

....

....

....

Tip

As you conduct research, different perspectives will impact your own personal perspective. For example, the global perspective you develop might not change your personal perspective, but it might strengthen it.

Peer feedback

3 Share your answers with your classmates.
Change or add to your answers in a different colour if necessary.

Independent reflection activity

What helped you to learn today?

....

How did you help someone else learn today?

....

Check your learning

If you haven't already done so, complete the **How will I know if I reach my goals?** table with 'Not there yet' or 'Achieved'. Don't forget to add examples from your challenge.

Developing analysis skills: Lesson 6

2.1 Identify ideas and evidence from different perspectives within different sources on a given topic

My learning goals are to develop my knowledge and understanding about:

- the difference between a global, a national and a personal perspective
- identifying and explaining different perspectives from an information source
- explaining my own personal perspective

How will I know if I reach my goals?

As you work through this lesson and you achieve your learning goals, tick the 'Achieved' box to show you have completed this. If you haven't quite achieved your learning goals, tick 'Not there yet'. Start to think about how you are going to show your learning goals in your challenge. Add an example from your challenge once you have achieved each learning goal.

Lesson 6	Not there yet	Achieved	Example
I know the difference between a global, national and personal perspective.			
I can identify and explain some different perspectives from an information source.			
I can explain my own personal perspective on an issue.			

Prior learning

1 Think about the topic you worked on in the Main activity in Lesson 5 to develop your skills. Complete these sentence starters:

I used to think ....

Now I think ....

because ....

2 Share your thinking with your partner. Has your partner's thinking changed or developed? How?

....

....

3 Is what you think considered as a global, national or personal perspective?

....

Starter activity

1 Look at the picture your teacher shows you.
What perspective does the picture show?

....

2 Explain why you think this.

....

....

3 Using what you've learnt from discussion about perspectives, tell your partner what you think the difference is between a global, a national and a personal perspective.

....

....

> **Tip**
>
> A global perspective may come from a specific country, organisation, institution, or even an individual, but it will have influence that spreads beyond any one country.

4 Do you think your partner understands the difference between a global, national and a personal perspective?   Yes/No

If not, how can you help them to understand the difference?

....

....

Main activity

The topic I am working on today is …

....

1 Look at the text your teacher gives you. Find some ideas and evidence for each of the perspectives in the table below. Discuss them with a partner. Make notes in the table.

Title of the text	
Global perspective	
National perspective	
Personal perspective	
Reference	

Peer feedback

2   Share your findings with your classmates.
    Add further ideas to your table in a different colour.

3   Choose one of the perspectives. Write a short paragraph
    to explain the perspective and your opinion of it.
    Do you agree with it? Why/Why not?

a   Perspective: ....

    ....

    ....

b   Your opinion of the perspective including why you do/do not
    agree with it: ....

    ....

    ....

    ....

Independent reflection activity

Using what you have learnt so far, are you developing your understanding of
the following:

A   A global perspective?   Yes/No

B   A national perspective?   Yes/No

C   A personal perspective?   Yes/No

Give an example for each:

A   A global perspective: ....

B   A national perspective: ....

C   A personal perspective: ....

Independent reflection activity

What do you now need to do to develop your understanding further?

....

....

Check your learning

If you haven't already done so, complete the **How will I know if I reach my goals?** table with 'Not there yet' or 'Achieved'. Don't forget to add examples from your challenge.

Self-assessment 2

Look back at self-assessment 1. How much further progress do you feel you have made so far in developing your analysis skills?

For each learning objective in the table below, shade in the response that matches yours most closely. Give one example for this response. Eventually, you are aiming for green!

Learning objectives: *to develop my knowledge and understanding about how to ...*	RED	AMBER	GREEN
2.1 Identify ideas and evidence from different perspectives within different sources on a given topic.	I can identify ideas and evidence from different perspectives within different sources with help. I can summarise different perspectives with help.	I can identify ideas and evidence from different perspectives within different sources. I can summarise different perspectives.	I can identify ideas and evidence from different perspectives within different sources. I can summarise different perspectives. I can help others summarise different perspectives.

Continued

Learning objectives: *to develop my knowledge and understanding about how to …*	RED	AMBER	GREEN
2.2 Explain how graphical or numerical data supports an argument.	I can identify relevant information from a graph with help. I can explain how graphs can be used as evidence to support an argument with help.	I can identify relevant information from a graph. I can explain how graphs can be used as evidence to support an argument.	I can identify relevant information from a graph. I can explain how graphs can be used as evidence to support an argument. I can help others recognise how graphs can be used as evidence to support an argument.
2.3 Explain causes of a local or global issue and consequences on others.	I can explain causes and consequences of an issue with help.	I can explain causes and consequences of an issue.	I can explain causes and consequences of an issue. I can help others explain causes and consequences of an issue.
2.4 Suggest and justify different actions to make a positive difference to a national or global issue.	I can ask some suitable questions to decide on a course of action with help. I can suggest at least one action to help resolve or make a positive difference to an issue with help.	I can ask some suitable questions to decide on a course of action. I can suggest at least one action to help resolve or make a positive difference to an issue.	I can ask some suitable questions to decide on a course of action. I can suggest different actions to help resolve or make a positive difference to an issue. I can help others to come up with different actions to help resolve or make a positive difference to an issue.

Continued

Examples:

2.1 ....

2.2 ....

2.3 ....

2.4 ....

Reflect on your responses in your self-assessment and identify two areas for improvement. Set yourself two learning targets – how you will improve upon the two areas. For example, 'I will try to come up with more than one course of action to make a positive difference to an issue.'

Learning targets:

1   Area for improvement: ....

    How I will improve: ....

2   Area for improvement: ....

    How I will improve: ....

Challenge topic review

Think about the challenge topic you have been exploring and complete the statements.

I was surprised to discover that ....

I didn't know ....

I now think ....

Getting better at analysis skills: Lesson 7

2.1 Identify ideas and evidence from different perspectives within different sources on a given topic

My learning goals are to get better at:

- understanding Global Perspectives key terms
- identifying different groups of stakeholders
- explaining the perspective of a group of stakeholders

How will I know if I reach my goals?

As you work through this lesson and you achieve your learning goals, tick the 'Achieved' box to show you have completed this. If you haven't quite achieved your learning goals, tick 'Not there yet'. Start to think about how you are going to show your learning goals in your challenge. Add an example from your challenge once you have achieved each learning goal.

Lesson 7	Not there yet	Achieved	Example
I understand some Global Perspectives key terms.			
I can identify different groups of stakeholders.			
I can explain the perspective of a group of stakeholders.			

Prior learning

Answer the quick quiz questions your teacher gives you.

1 ....

....

2 ....

....

3 ....

....

4 ....

....

5 ....

....

Starter activity

Class discussion

1 After class discussion about answers to the questions in the Prior learning activity, write down all five questions and answers.

1 ....

....

2 ....

....

3 ....

....

4 ....

....

5 ....

....

2 Discuss the list with a partner. Write down five further questions with answers.

1 ....

....

2 ....

....

3 ....

....

4 ....

....

5 ....

....

3 Ask your questions to another pair to check they know the answers.

Did they get all the answers to the questions right?   Yes/No

Which one(s) did they get wrong?

....

Why do you think this was?

....

Main activity

The topic I am working on today is …

....

1   Look at the issue your teacher shows you. Write the issue in the middle of the diagram. Brainstorm all the groups of people who might have an interest in this issue. Add as many circles and arrows to the diagram as you need to record your ideas.

Tip

A group of people who share common knowledge and values that influence their perspective are called stakeholders.

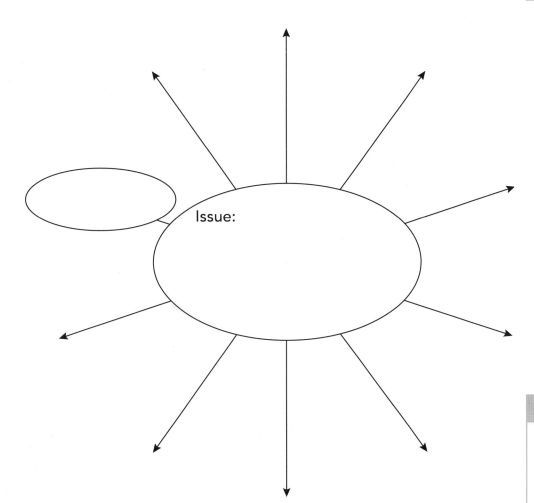

Issue:

Tip

A stakeholder is someone with a vested interested in a topic/issue. The topic/issue affects them somehow.

2 **a** Choose one of the groups of people from your diagram.

....

b Discuss the chosen group in your team. Summarise what perspective you think this group of stakeholders might have on the issue.

....

....

....

Peer feedback

3 Share your summary with your classmates.
Add any further ideas to your summary.

....

....

Tip

There will be different perspectives within a group of stakeholders. For example, learners could make up a group of stakeholders, but it is likely that learners in Grade 7 will have a different perspective about a topic to learners in Grade 10.

Independent reflection activity

What have you done well today?

....

What skills have you used today?

....

Check your learning

If you haven't already done so, complete the **How will I know if I reach my goals?** table with 'Not there yet' or 'Achieved'. Don't forget to add examples from your challenge.

8

Getting better at analysis skills: Lesson 8

2.1 Identify ideas and evidence from different perspectives within different sources on a given topic

2.2 Explain how graphical or numerical data supports an argument

My learning goals are to get better at:

- giving examples of different groups of stakeholders
- finding ideas and evidence from different perspectives
- asking questions to gain information from a specific group of people

How will I know if I reach my goals?

As you work through this lesson and you achieve your learning goals, tick the 'Achieved' box to show you have completed this. If you haven't quite achieved your learning goals, tick 'Not there yet'. Start to think about how you are going to show your learning goals in your challenge. Add an example from your challenge once you have achieved each learning goal.

Lesson 8	Not there yet	Achieved	Example
I can give examples of different groups of stakeholders.			
I can find ideas and evidence from different perspectives.			
I can ask questions to gain information from a specific group of people.			

Prior learning

1   What do you think is meant by the term 'stakeholder'? Discuss it with a partner. Write your definition.

A stakeholder is ....

2   Give three examples of stakeholders for the issue you worked on in the Main activity in Lesson 7.

a   ....

b   ....

c   ....

3   Do you think each of the groups of stakeholders in task **2** will have the same perspective? Explain your answer.

....

....

The topic I am working on today is ...

....

Starter activity

Look at the text your teacher has given you.

1   What perspective is suggested in the text?

....

2   What other groups of people might be affected by or have an interest in this issue?

....

....

> **Tip**
>
> When trying to deepen your understanding of an issue, you need to look for groups of people with an interest in the issue whose perspective is likely to be different.

3 How might the perspective of each of the groups in your answer to task **2** be different?

....

....

4 How might you find out information about each perspective?

....

....

5 Share your ideas with your classmates.

Main activity

1 Design a questionnaire to gain information about the issue your teacher gives you.

What questions are you going to ask?

1 ....

2 ....

3 ....

4 ....

5 ....

6 ....

7 ....

8 ....

9 ....

10 ....

Tip

Questions with a 'Yes' or 'No' answer are closed questions. They are easy to analyse. You can present your findings as a graph.

Tip

Open-ended questions that require more than a 'Yes' or 'No' answer allow you to gain more information, which you can summarise in a paragraph.

Tip

Open-ended questions often start with 'Why?' or 'How?'

Tip

An example of an open-ended question is, 'Why do you think young people like social media?'

2 Ask for feedback on your questionnaire from your teacher.
Make improvements to your questions.

3 Design your questionnaire on a separate piece of paper and give it to
a group of 5–10 Stage 8 learners to gain a perspective from them.

Independent reflection activity

What did you find easy in today's lesson?

....

What did you need help with in today's lesson?

....

Check your learning

If you haven't already done so, complete the **How will I know if I reach my goals?** table
with 'Not there yet' or 'Achieved'. Don't forget to add examples from your challenge.

Getting better at analysis skills: Lesson 9

2.1 Identify ideas and evidence from different perspectives within different sources on a given topic

2.2 Explain how graphical or numerical data supports an argument

2.3 Explain causes of a local or global issue and consequences on others

2.4 Suggest and justify different actions to make a positive difference to a national or global issue

My learning goals are to get better at:

- using data from research into different perspectives on an issue to help support an argument
- explaining consequences of a local or national issue
- suggesting an action to make a positive difference to a local or national issue

How will I know if I reach my goals?

As you work through this lesson and you achieve your learning goals, tick the 'Achieved' box to show you have completed this. If you haven't quite achieved your learning goals, tick 'Not there yet'. Start to think about how you are going to show your learning goals in your challenge. Add an example from your challenge once you have achieved each learning goal.

Lesson 9	Not there yet	Achieved	Example
I can use data from research to help support an argument.			
I can explain the consequences of a local or national issue.			
I can suggest an action to make a positive difference to a local or national issue.			

Prior learning

In teams, discuss your research findings from your questionnaire in Lesson 8.

1 What did you find out?

....

2 What did the majority think about the issue(s)?

....

3 Was there a difference between the opinion of boys and girls?

....

4 Did you get the results you thought you would get? Why do you think that was?

....

5 Were there any surprises? If so, what were they?

....

6 What conclusions can you draw?

....

....

The topic I am working on today is …

....

Starter activity

Discuss an issue from your questionnaire with your team and make notes below.

a Your issue: ....

b Information gained from your research: ....

....

c Is further research needed to gain a different perspective?   Yes/No

d If yes, what is your proposed course of action for taking different perspectives into account?

....

....

....

Main activity

Continuing from the Starter activity, do further research on your issue if necessary. After discussion about the issue and course of action, make notes below.

a Course of action:

....

b Reason(s) for this course of action:

....

....

c Notes from research to include in the outcome:

....

....

....

....

....

Tip

A course of action needs an outcome, e.g. a presentation, leaflet or poster promoting something or raising awareness about something to help make a positive difference.

Tip

A course of action needs to be related to an issue. A local issue will need a local course of action.

Tip

An example for a local course of action might be to raise awareness about the need to save water. An outcome to do this might be a presentation to classmates in school.

Independent reflection activity

What skills have you used in today's lesson?

....

How might you further develop these skills?

....

Check your learning

If you haven't already done so, complete the **How will I know if I reach my goals?** table with 'Not there yet' or 'Achieved'. Don't forget to add examples from your challenge.

Self-assessment 3

Look back at self-assessment 1 and 2. How much further progress do you feel you have made so far in developing your analysis skills?

For each learning objective in the table below, shade in the response that matches yours most closely. Give one example for this response. Eventually, you are aiming for green!

Learning objectives: *to get better at understanding how to . . .*	RED	AMBER	GREEN
2.1 Identify ideas and evidence from different perspectives within different sources on a given topic.	I know one or two Global Perspectives key terms. I can identify some different groups of stakeholders with help. I can explain the perspective of a group of stakeholders with help.	I know some Global Perspectives key terms. I can identify some different groups of stakeholders. I can explain the perspective of a group of stakeholders.	I know key Global Perspectives key terms. I can identify different groups of stakeholders. I can explain the perspective of a group of stakeholders. I can help others identify stakeholders and explain their perspective.

Continued

Learning objectives: *to get better at understanding how to . . .*	RED	AMBER	GREEN
2.2 Explain how graphical or numerical data supports an argument.	I can find relevant information on the internet with help. I can ask some questions (although they may not all be relevant) to gain some information to help support an argument.	I can find relevant information on the internet. I can ask questions to gain some information to help support an argument.	I can find relevant information on the internet. I can ask questions to gain information to help support an argument. I can help others ask questions to gain relevant information to help support an argument.
2.3 Explain causes of a local or global issue and consequences on others.	I can explain at least one cause or consequence of a local or national issue with help.	I can explain some causes or consequences of a local or national issue using appropriate signal words.	I can explain some causes and consequences of a local or national issue using appropriate signal words and can help others understand how to explain causes and consequences.
2.4 Suggest and justify different actions to make a positive difference to a national or global issue.	I can suggest at least one possible course of action to help make a positive difference to a local or national issue with help.	I can suggest a relevant course of action and at least one outcome to help make a positive difference to a local or national issue.	I can suggest relevant courses of action and different outcomes to help make a positive difference to a local or national issue. I can help others come up with relevant courses of action and suggestions for outcomes.

Continued

Examples:

2.1 ....

2.2 ....

2.3 ....

2.4 ....

Reflect on your responses in your self-assessment and identify two areas for improvement. Set yourself two learning targets – how you will improve upon the two areas. For example, 'I will try to help someone else think of a suitable outcome to help make a positive difference to a local or national issue.'

Learning targets:

1   Area for improvement: ....

    How I will improve: ....

2   Area for improvement: ....

    How I will improve: ....

Challenge topic review

Think about the challenge topic you have been exploring and complete the statements.

I was surprised to discover that ....

I didn't know ....

I now think ....

Evaluation

This section of your Learner's Skills Book 8 helps you to develop your evaluation skills using interesting global topics.

Starting with . . .

As you start to develop your evaluation skills in Stage 8, you will be explaining what the term 'evaluation' means and gaining a deeper understanding of the difference between evaluation and analysis. You will learn how to evaluate sources of information, consider the author and purpose of the source and check whether the sources contain bias. You will discuss how to recognise a 'fake news' item and learn to recognise that some facts in information sources are real and some are made up.

Developing . . .

As you further develop your evaluation skills in Stage 8, you will discuss the effectiveness of different sources of information on a variety of global issues. You will be learning what an argument in Global Perspectives is and how to create an argument by exploring what a claim is, giving reasons for a claim and using different sources of information as evidence to support your claims. You will also continue to evaluate sources of information to decide whether they are reliable or not, or if and why they might contain bias.

Getting better at . . .

As you get better at evaluating in Stage 8, you will continue to evaluate different information sources – including ideas and evidence from different perspectives – considering the author and purpose of different text types. You will get better at judging the reliability of sources, furthering your understanding that some sources may contain bias.

1

Starting with evaluation skills: Lesson 1

3.1 Evaluate sources, considering the author and purpose, recognising that some sources may be biased

My learning goals are to start to:

- explain the term 'evaluation'

- understand the difference between evaluation and analysis

- understand what 'fake news' is, why it is created and how to recognise it

How will I know if I reach my goals?

As you work through this lesson and you achieve your learning goals, tick the 'Achieved' box to show you have completed this. If you haven't quite achieved your learning goals, tick 'Not there yet'. Start to think about how you are going to show your learning goals in your challenge. Add an example from your challenge once you have achieved each learning goal.

Lesson 1	Not there yet	Achieved	Example
I can explain the term 'evaluation'.			
I understand the difference between evaluation and analysis.			
I understand what 'fake news' is, why it is created and how to recognise it.			

Prior learning

1 Answer these questions:

   a   What do you do in Global Perspectives lessons?

   ....

   b   Who do you work with in Global Perspectives lessons?

   ....

   c   When are your Global Perspectives lessons?

   ....

   d   Do you like what you do in Global Perspectives lessons?   Yes/No?

   Why/Why not? ....

   e   Do you think Global Perspectives lessons can be improved? How?

   ....

2 Which of the questions in task **1** do you think ask you to analyse
   Global Perspectives lessons and which ask you to evaluate them?

   ....

3 Do your classmates agree?   Yes/No

4 Using what you've learnt from class discussion, write a definition in no more
   than ten words for each of the terms 'analysis' and 'evaluation'.

   Analysis ....

   ....

   Evaluation ....

   ....

Starter activity

1 Which one of the following statements is not an evaluation?

   A It is a bit outdated as it was written in 2010.

   B The argument cites expert views.

   C The article is biased because the author works for the company.

   D It is a bit one-sided.

   E This is due to advances in technology.

   F Factual evidence is lacking.

   G It uses a lot of good examples.

2 Share your ideas to see if your classmates agree.

3 Are you becoming more confident in knowing what the term 'evaluation' means and how it differs from analysis?   Yes/No

   How are you going to (further) develop this confidence?

   ....

The topic I am working on today is …

....

Main activity

1 Discuss the following questions with a partner.
   Then write down the answers.

   a What is fake news?

   ....

   b Why is fake news created?

   ....

   ....

   c Why does fake news matter?

   ....

> **Tip**
>
> To cite something means to refer to a text, book or author as evidence to help support an argument.

> **Tip**
>
> A biased author may not present all the facts or develop a reasoned argument to support their opinion(s). For example, someone in favour of technological advancement is unlikely to give the disadvantages of digital technologies.

> **Tip**
>
> Good examples are ones that come from well-known sources such as the United Nations or the World Health Organization.

d Do you think that your teacher generally gives you fake news items?   Yes/No

Why/Why not?

....

2 Look at the news item your teacher shows you. Discuss it with a partner.

a Do you think the news item is real or fake?

....

b Why do you think this?

....

....

3 Do your classmates agree?   Yes/No

Class discussion

4 After class discussion, write down what to look for to be able to judge if a news item is fake.

....

....

....

....

....

> **Tip**
>
> A one-sided argument does not present all the evidence, e.g. describing the advantages of digital technology but not the disadvantages.

> **Tip**
>
> When evaluating a news item, try to give reasons why you think it might be real or fake.

> **Tip**
>
> To evaluate a source, you need to give its strengths and weaknesses.

Tip

The term 'fake news' is given to false information that is deliberately created to trick people into believing it is true and is often created for political or business reasons.

Independent reflection activity

Which part of today's lesson did you find the most difficult?

....

Why do you think this was?

....

What skills have you used today?

....

Check your learning

If you haven't already done so, complete the **How will I know if I reach my goals?** table with 'Not there yet' or 'Achieved'. Don't forget to add examples from your challenge.

Starting with evaluation skills: Lesson 2

3.1 Evaluate sources, considering the author and purpose, recognising that some sources may be biased

My learning goals are to start to:

- recognise that facts from news stories can be real or fake
- understand how to judge if a fact is real or fake

How will I know if I reach my goals?

As you work through this lesson and you achieve your learning goals, tick the 'Achieved' box to show you have completed this. If you haven't quite achieved your learning goals, tick 'Not there yet'. Start to think about how you are going to show your learning goals in your challenge. Add an example from your challenge once you have achieved each learning goal.

Lesson 2	Not there yet	Achieved	Example
I recognise that facts from news stories can be real or fake.			
I know how to judge if a fact in an information source is real or fake.			

Prior learning

1 Answer these questions:

a What is meant by the word 'news'?

....

b What is meant by the term 'fake news'?

....

c Why do people create 'fake news'?

....

2 Using what you have learnt from class discussion about 'news' and 'fake news', add to your answers in a different colour.

Starter activity

1 Look at the news headlines your teacher shows you. Discuss them with a partner. Do you think the headlines are real or fake? Why?

a ....

b ....

c ....

2 How could you check if the headlines in task **1** are real or fake?

....

The topic I am working on today is …

....

Main activity

1 a Work with a partner. Find a popular news story and write down the title/headline.

....

b In this news story, find and write down an interesting piece of information that looks like a fact.

....

c Find the supposed fact that you found in task **b** in more than one other information source. List the sources.

....

....

d What purpose does this supposed fact serve?

....

e How do you know if the supposed fact from task **b** is true?

....

f Do you know what the original source for the supposed fact from task **b** was? If not, how might you find out?

....

g Now find and write down a supposed fact from the original news story in task **a**, which is in just this one information source and that you cannot find anywhere else.

....

h How might you work out if the supposed fact in task **g** is real or fake?

....

> **Tip**
>
> A fact is a thing that is known to be true or has been proven to be true. Facts do not always need to be statistics; they can be statements.

> **Tip**
>
> If a piece of information that looks like a fact is actually fake, it's likely you will never have heard of the website it's reported on.

> **Tip**
>
> Try to search for the supposed fact in more than one information source to check if it's true or not.

Peer feedback

2 Use this checklist to give feedback on the supposed fact found by another pair. You can write notes on where they found the 'fact', the purpose it serves, what you can find out about the person reporting the 'fact', etc.

	Checklist	Yes/No	Notes
1	Has the fact been reported anywhere else?		
2	Is it on the radio, TV or in the newspapers?		
3	Have you heard of the author/ organisation that published the fact?		
4	Does the information source where you found the fact look real?		
5	Does the fact serve a specific purpose?		
6	Does the fact sound believable?		
7	Is the author reporting the fact a real person?		
8	Is there anything odd about the information source the fact is in?		

Independent reflection activity

Which part of this lesson did you find difficult? Why?

....

....

How have you used research skills today?

....

Check your learning

If you haven't already done so, complete the **How will I know if I reach my goals?** table with 'Not there yet' or 'Achieved'. Don't forget to add examples from your challenge.

3

Starting with evaluation skills: Lesson 3

3.1 Evaluate sources, considering the author and purpose, recognising that some sources may be biased

3.2 Discuss the effectiveness of a source, making explicit reference to its development of an argument

---

My learning goals are to start to:

- recognise that some facts in a news story might not be true
- identify bias in a source
- realise that news stories may contain bias
- realise that the argument in a source should make sense if it is to be trusted

---

How will I know if I reach my goals?

As you work through this lesson and you achieve your learning goals, tick the 'Achieved' box to show you have completed this. If you haven't quite achieved your learning goals, tick 'Not there yet'. Start to think about how you are going to show your learning goals in your challenge. Add an example from your challenge once you have achieved each learning goal.

Lesson 3	Not there yet	Achieved	Example
I know some ways of telling whether supposed facts in a news story are untrue.			
I can identify bias in a source.			
I realise that news stories may contain bias.			
I realise that the argument in a source should make sense if it is be trusted.			

Prior learning

1 How do you check if information that looks like a fact in a source is real or fake? Discuss with a partner.

....

2 Check with another pair. Do they agree or have different ideas?

....

Starter activity

1 Refer to the news story in the Main activity in Lesson 2. Discuss it with a partner.

2 On a separate piece of paper, write the story in your own words, using only facts from the trusted information sources you found in Lesson 2.

3 Swap stories with another pair to see if you can find the sources they used. List them here.

....

....

> **Tip**
>
> A reliable source of information is a source that can be trusted to be true.

The topic I am working on today is …

....

Main activity

1 Look at the information source your teacher shows you. Make notes about the main idea and the facts.

Main idea: ....

Facts: ....

....

> **Tip**
>
> An unreliable source is a source that cannot be trusted to be true.

2 Discuss the story in the source with a partner. Complete the checklist, expanding on your answers in the Notes column.

	Checklist	Yes	No	Notes
1	Has the story been reported anywhere else?			
2	Is the purpose of the story clear?			
3	Have you heard of the organisation that published the story?			
4	Does the story sound believable?			
5	Is the argument in the story logical?			
6	Are there any errors in spelling or grammar (in text only)?			
7	Is the author of the story a real person?			
8	Is there anything odd about the date the story was published?			
9	Does the story contain bias?			
10	Is there any other evidence to support the story?			

3 a Do you think this information source is real or fake? ....

   b Why? ....

      ....

4 What does your partner think?

....

Class discussion

5 a Using what you have learnt from class discussion about real and fake news, do you feel more confident about judging if an information source is real or fake? Why?

Yes, because ....

No, because ....

b What would help you further?

....

Independent reflection activity

What skills have you used today?

....

....

What has helped you to learn today?

....

....

Check your learning

If you haven't already done so, complete the **How will I know if I reach my goals?** table with 'Not there yet' or 'Achieved'. Don't forget to add examples from your challenge.

> **Tip**
>
> It is most likely that you will have heard of the more reliable sources of information, e.g. newspapers such as *The Guardian* and *Hindustani Times*, news agencies like the BBC and Al Jazeera, and global organisations such as the United Nations and the WWF (World Wide Fund for Nature).

Self-assessment 1

How much progress do you feel you have made so far in developing your evaluation skills?

For each learning objective in the table below, shade in the response that matches yours most closely. Give one example for this response. Eventually, you are aiming for green!

Learning objectives: to start to . . .	RED	AMBER	GREEN
3.1 Evaluate sources, considering the author and purpose, recognising that some sources may be biased.	I can explain what evaluation is with help. I understand what fake news is and can recognise it with help. I can check if facts in an information source are real or fake with help.	I can explain what evaluation is. I understand what fake news is and can recognise it. I can check if facts in an information source are real or fake.	I can explain what evaluation is and understand the difference between evaluation and analysis. I understand what fake news is and can recognise it. I can check if facts in an information source are real or fake and can help others check the reliability of sources of information.
3.2 Discuss the effectiveness of a source, making explicit reference to its development of an argument.	I understand that bias can affect the effectiveness of an information source. I can recognise bias in an information source with help. I can recognise an argument that does not make sense with help.	I understand that bias can affect the effectiveness of an information source. I can recognise bias in an information source. I can recognise arguments that do and do not make sense.	I understand that bias can affect the effectiveness of an information source. I can recognise bias in an information source. I can recognise arguments that do and do not make sense and help others recognise arguments that don't make sense.

Continued

Examples:

3.1 ....

3.2 ....

Reflect on your responses in your self-assessment and identify two areas for improvement. Set yourself two learning targets – how you will improve upon the two areas. For example, 'I will check that the facts I use in my work are true by looking for them in different information sources.'

Learning targets:

1   Area for improvement: ....

   How I will improve: ....

2   Area for improvement: ....

   How I will improve: ....

Challenge topic review

Think about the challenge topic you have been exploring and complete the statements.

I was surprised to discover that ....

I didn't know ....

I now think ....

4

Developing evaluation skills: Lesson 4

3.2 Discuss the effectiveness of a source, making explicit reference to its development of an argument

How will I know if I reach my goals?

As you work through this lesson and you achieve your learning goals, tick the 'Achieved' box to show you have completed this. If you haven't quite achieved your learning goals, tick 'Not there yet'. Start to think about how you are going to show your learning goals in your challenge. Add an example from your challenge once you have achieved each learning goal.

Lesson 4	Not there yet	Achieved	Example
I can explain what an argument is in Global Perspectives.			
I can explain what makes an effective argument.			
I can explain how to write an argument.			

1   What do you think the term 'argument' means in Global Perspectives?
    Discuss this with a partner.

    ....

2   Do your classmates agree?   Yes/No

3   Use what you have learnt from class discussion. Now explain to someone who
    doesn't know what you do in Global Perspectives lessons what an argument is.
    Use less than ten words.

    ....

    ....

The topic I am working on today is …

....

Starter activity

Look at the picture your teacher shows you.

1   Write down three claims related to the photo.

    1   ....

    2   ....

    3   ....

Class discussion

2   After class discussion, write down three further claims.

    1   ....

    2   ....

    3   ....

Tip

A claim is a statement or assertion that something is true, typically without providing supporting evidence or proof.

Tip

A claim answers the question What do I think? For example, 'Having different cultures in a city encourages tolerance amongst all people.'

3 Using what you've learnt from giving examples of claims, what do you think a claim is?

A claim is ....

....

4 Does your partner agree?   Yes/No

Main activity

1 Look at the text your teacher gives you. Discuss it with a partner and then answer the questions.

a What is the author's claim?

....

b What reasons and evidence does the author use to support their claim?

Reasons: ....

....

Evidence: ....

....

c Do you think the argument is convincing?   Yes/No

d Why?/Why not?

....

....

> **Tip**
>
> An argument in Global Perspectives is a reason or set of reasons to justify a claim, perspective or action, and is usually supported by evidence.

> **Tip**
>
> A reason answers the question: Why do I think this? For example, '. . . because you realise that they have the same interest as you even though they live in a different culture.'

> **Tip**
>
> Evidence answers the question: How do I know this? For example, 'A report in *The Telegraph* suggests everyone should live abroad at least once in their life.'

Independent reflection activity

What skills have you used in today's lesson?

....

Are you starting to get a better understanding of what an argument is?   Yes/No

Complete this statement:

An argument is made up of ....

....

Check your learning

If you haven't already done so, complete the **How will I know if I reach my goals?** table with 'Not there yet' or 'Achieved'. Don't forget to add examples from your challenge.

Developing evaluation skills: Lesson 5

3.2 Discuss the effectiveness of a source, making explicit reference to its development of an argument

My learning goals are to develop my knowledge and understanding about:

- identifying claims
- identifying reasoning to justify a claim
- identifying evidence in support of a claim

How will I know if I reach my goals?

As you work through this lesson and you achieve your learning goals, tick the 'Achieved' box to show you have completed this. If you haven't quite achieved your learning goals, tick 'Not there yet'. Start to think about how you are going to show your learning goals in your challenge. Add an example from your challenge once you have achieved each learning goal.

Lesson 5	Not there yet	Achieved	Example
I can identify a claim.			
I can identify reasoning to justify a claim.			
I can identify evidence in support of a claim.			

Prior learning

1   Which of these questions can you ask to identify a claim?

    A   Why does the author think this?

    B   How does the author know this?

    C   What does the author think?

    ....

    Did you choose the same as your partner?   Yes/No

2   What might you be able to identify by asking the other two questions in task **1**?

    ....

    ....

3   Discuss the terms below with a partner. Give an example for each.

    Claim: ....

    Reason: ....

    Evidence: ....

The topic I am working on today is …

....

Starter activity

1   Watch the video clip your teacher shows you. Then write down:

    a   one claim in the video: ....

    ....

    b   reason(s) for the claim: ....

    ....

Tip

Evidence is anything that can support or back up a claim, e.g. a scientific report, a study or a quotation from someone or something that someone has read.

c   evidence to support the claim: ....

....

2   Check to see if your classmates have the same.
Add any further ideas in a different colour.

Tip

Reasons should justify the claim made, e.g. the idea of missing family and friends does not justify the claim, 'Young people love living in a new country.'

Main activity

1   Find an interesting text. Then write down:

a   the text reference: ....

b   one claim in the text: ....

....

c   reason(s) for the claim: ....

....

d   one piece of evidence to support the claim: ....

....

Peer feedback

2   Share your work with someone else. Give feedback to each other
by answering the questions. Then make changes to your own work
if need be.

a   Is the text reference correct?   Yes/No

....

b   Do you understand the claim?   Yes/No

....

....

Tip

A claim is often used as a headline for a news story, e.g. 'Two-thirds of young people in the United Kingdom are considering moving abroad.'

    c   Does the reasoning justify the claim?   Yes/No

....

....

    d   Does the evidence support the claim?   Yes/No

....

....

Independent reflection activity

What helped you to learn today?

....

How did you help someone else learn today?

....

What skills have you used today?

....

Check your learning

If you haven't already done so, complete the **How will I know if I reach my goals?** table with 'Not there yet' or 'Achieved'. Don't forget to add examples from your challenge.

6

Developing evaluation skills: Lesson 6

3.1 Evaluate sources, considering the author and purpose, recognising that some sources may be biased

My learning goals are to develop my knowledge and understanding about:

- the meaning of the term 'bias' and judging if a text contains any bias
- the purpose of different texts
- the audience for different texts

How will I know if I reach my goals?

As you work through this lesson and you achieve your learning goals, tick the 'Achieved' box to show you have completed this. If you haven't quite achieved your learning goals, tick 'Not there yet'. Start to think about how you are going to show your learning goals in your challenge. Add an example from your challenge once you have achieved each learning goal.

Lesson 6	Not there yet	Achieved	Example
I understand the meaning of the term 'bias'.			
I can judge if a text contains bias.			
I can identify the purpose of a text.			
I can identify the audience for a text.			

Prior learning

1 What does the term 'bias' mean to you? Discuss it with a partner.

....

....

2 Share your definition of bias with another pair. Do they agree?
Make changes to your definition in a different colour.

3 After class discussion, explain what bias is and give an example.

Bias is ....

....

An example of bias ....

....

The topic I am working on today is …

....

Starter activity

1 Look at the video clips your teacher shows you.
Discuss them with a partner. What is the purpose of each clip?

a ....

b ....

c ....

2 Do the video clips contain bias? Discuss with a partner.
Explain your answer.

a ....

b ....

c ....

Tip

Bias is a judgment based on a personal point of view. People who are biased often believe what they want to believe, refusing to take different perspectives or the opinions of others into consideration.

3 Do your classmates agree with your answers? Yes/No

If not, which answers do they disagree with?

....

....

The topic I am working on today is …

....

Main activity

1 Look at the text titles your teacher shows you. Write them down.

A ....

B ....

C ....

2 Discuss the text titles with a partner.
Answer the following questions about each text title.

a Which audience do you think each text is aimed at?

A ....

B ....

C ....

b What do you think the purpose of each text is?

A ....

B ....

C ....

> **Tip**
>
> Different types of text are created for different purposes. Texts can entertain, persuade, advise, argue, describe, inform and instruct. For example, a recipe for a meal instructs you how to create the meal.

> **Tip**
>
> Different texts are aimed at different people. For example, a tourist guide of a town is aimed at people who are interested in visiting particular places in that town and a joke book is aimed at people who want a laugh.

c Do you think each text will contain bias? Why/Why not?

A ....

B ....

C ....

3 Share your answers to task **2** with another pair. Do they agree?

Class discussion

4 Using what you have learnt from class discussion, what do you think the titles of texts can tell us?

....

....

Independent reflection activity

Think about your learning today. Complete these sentence stems:

I used to think ....

But now I think ....

Because ....

Has your partner's thinking changed or developed?   Yes/No

Why? ....

....

Check your learning

If you haven't already done so, complete the **How will I know if I reach my goals?** table with 'Not there yet' or 'Achieved'. Don't forget to add examples from your challenge.

Self-assessment 2

Look back at self-assessment 1. How much further progress do you feel you have made so far in developing your evaluation skills?

For each learning objective in the table below, shade in the response that matches yours most closely. Give one example for this response. Eventually, you are aiming for green!

Learning objectives: *to develop my knowledge and understanding about how to . . .*	RED	AMBER	GREEN
3.1 Evaluate sources, considering the author and purpose, recognising that some sources may be biased.	I can explain what evaluation is. I can recognise if an information source might contain bias with help. I can identify the audience for and purpose of different texts with help.	I can explain what evaluation is. I can recognise if an information source might contain bias. I can identify the audience for and purpose of different texts.	I can explain what evaluation is. I can recognise if an information source might contain bias. I can identify the audience for and purpose of different texts. I can help others identify the audience for and purpose of a text and recognise if an information source might contain bias.
3.2 Discuss the effectiveness of a source, making explicit reference to its development of an argument.	I can recognise the characteristics of an argument in Global Perspectives with help. I can identify some of the features of an effective argument with help. I can attempt to write an argument with help.	I can recognise the characteristics of an argument in Global Perspectives. I can identify the features of an effective argument. I can write an argument with some help.	I can recognise the characteristics of an argument in Global Perspectives. I can identify the features of an effective argument. I can write an effective argument and help others write an effective argument.

Continued

Examples:

3.1 ....

3.2 ....

Reflect on your responses in your self-assessment and identify two areas for improvement. Set yourself two learning targets – how you will improve upon the two areas. For example, 'I will check that my argument has a claim and at least one reason and one piece of evidence to support my claim.'

Learning targets:

1   Area for improvement: ....

    How I will improve: ....

2   Area for improvement: ....

    How I will improve: ....

Challenge topic review

Think about the challenge topic you have been exploring and complete the following statements.

I was surprised to discover that ....

I didn't know ....

I now think ....

Getting better at evaluation skills: Lesson 7

3.1 Evaluate sources, considering the author and purpose, recognising that some sources may be biased

3.2 Discuss the effectiveness of a source, making explicit reference to its development of an argument

---

My learning goals are to get better at:

- understanding the difference between audience and purpose
- recognising fact and opinion
- recognising bias

How will I know if I reach my goals?

As you work through this lesson and you achieve your learning goals, tick the 'Achieved' box to show you have completed this. If you haven't quite achieved your learning goals, tick 'Not there yet'. Start to think about how you are going to show your learning goals in your challenge. Add an example from your challenge once you have achieved each learning goal.

Lesson 7	Not there yet	Achieved	Example
I know the difference between audience and purpose.			
I can recognise fact and opinion.			
I can recognise bias.			

Prior learning

1   What is the difference between the audience of a text and the purpose for a text? Discuss with a partner.

   a   Audience: ....

   b   Purpose: ....

2   Give an example for each.

   a   Audience: ....

   b   Purpose: ....

Starter activity

1   Discuss the following questions with a partner and then write down your answers.

   a   What is a claim?

   ....

   b   What types of evidence can help support a claim?

   ....

Peer feedback

2   Share your ideas with your classmates. Do they have further ideas for task **1**? Add them to your ideas in a different colour.

Class discussion

3   Using what you've learnt from class discussion about evidence, write down a definition for the terms 'fact' and 'opinion'.

   a   Fact: ....

   b   Opinion: ....

4 Do your classmates have the same definitions as you?
Make any changes in a different colour.

The topic I am working on today is …

....

Main activity

1 Using the text your teacher gives you, complete the following tasks.
Discuss with a partner.

   a Write down one claim.

     ....

   b Give a reason for this claim.

     ....

   c Give three pieces of evidence in the text.

     1 ....

     2 ....

     3 ....

   d Give one perspective and say why you think it is this perspective.

     Perspective: ....

     Reason: ....

   e Give one example of bias and say why you think it is bias.

     Bias: ....

     Reason: ....

2 How effective do you think the text is? Why?

....

....

Tip

A claim is a statement or assertion that something is true.

Tip

Reasoning and evidence are needed to justify a claim.

Tip

A perspective is a certain view about or attitude towards a topic, sub-topic or issue.

Tip

Bias is a judgment based on a personal point of view.

Tip

Bias can be seen as favouring a certain side.

Peer feedback

3   Give feedback to someone else in your class.
Then, ask that classmate to give you feedback in the box below.

You understand . . .	Yes	Not yet	Action
what a claim is			
what reasoning is			
what evidence is			
what a perspective is			
what bias is.			

> **Tip**
>
> A fact can be used as evidence and is something that can be proven to be true.

> **Tip**
>
> An opinion can be used as evidence but is something that cannot be proven;
> it's what someone thinks, so it is weaker evidence than a fact.

> **Independent reflection activity**
>
> What skill did you improve today?
>
> ....
>
> How did you improve it?
>
> ....

Check your learning

If you haven't already done so, complete the **How will I know if I reach my goals?** table with 'Not there yet' or 'Achieved'. Don't forget to add examples from your challenge.

Self-assessment 3

Look back at self-assessments 1 and 2. How much further progress do you feel you have made so far in developing your evaluation skills?

For each learning objective in the table below, shade in the response that matches yours most closely. Give one example for this response. Eventually, you are aiming for green!

Learning objectives: *to get better at understanding how to . . .*	RED	AMBER	GREEN
3.1 Evaluate sources, considering the author and purpose, recognising that some sources may be biased.	I can explain what evaluation is. I can recognise bias in an information source with help. I can identify the audience for and purpose of different texts with help.	I can explain what evaluation is. I can recognise bias in an information source. I can identify the audience for and purpose of different texts.	I can explain what evaluation is. I can recognise bias in an information source. I can identify the audience for and purpose of different texts. I can help others identify the audience for and purpose of a text and recognise bias.
3.2 Discuss the effectiveness of a source, making explicit reference to its development of an argument.	I can recognise the characteristics of an argument in Global Perspectives with help. I can identify some of the features of an effective argument with help. I can recognise different types of evidence with help.	I can recognise the characteristics of an argument in Global Perspectives. I can identify the features of an effective argument. I can recognise different types of evidence.	I can recognise the characteristics of an argument in Global Perspectives. I can identify the features of an effective argument. I can recognise different types of evidence and help others decide on the effectiveness of an information source.

Continued

Examples:

3.1 ....

3.2 ....

Reflect on your responses in your self-assessment and identify two areas for improvement. Set yourself two learning targets – how you will improve upon the two areas. For example, 'I will ask my teacher to show me more examples of bias so that I really understand what it is and how to recognise it.'

Learning targets:

1   Area for improvement: ....

    How I will improve: ....

2   Area for improvement: ....

    How I will improve: ....

Challenge topic review

Think about the challenge topic you have been exploring and complete the following statements.

I was surprised to discover that ....

I didn't know ....

I now think ....

Reflection

This section of your Learner's Skills Book 8 helps you to develop your reflection skills using interesting global topics.

Starting with . . .

As you start to develop your reflection skills in Stage 8, you will be deepening your learning about what reflection is in Global Perspectives and how it differs from evaluation. You will be identifying and explaining your own and others' personal strengths and weaknesses and identifying and explaining any areas for development. You will work in a team to produce a shared outcome, and gain feedback on this outcome. You will then reflect on the benefits and challenges of teamwork and your personal perspective about a global topic.

Developing . . .

As you further develop your reflection skills in Stage 8, you will work in a team to produce a set of questions for others to answer. Then you will reflect on your own and others' contributions to teamwork and any improvements you need to make for more effective teamwork to take place. You will also develop your knowledge and understanding about what a personal perspective is in Global Perspectives and reflect on how your personal perspective might develop or change as a result of research.

Getting better at . . .

As you get better at reflection in Stage 8, you will continue working with others towards producing a shared outcome. You will explore your contributions to teamwork and how these relate to your personal strengths. You will also consider any improvements you might make when contributing to teamwork. You will be better able to explain how your personal perspective has changed or developed according to the issue investigated, supporting your personal perspective with evidence.

Starting with reflection skills: Lesson 1

4.1 Explain personal contribution to teamwork and identify targets for improvement

4.4 Identify skills learnt or improved during an activity and relate to personal strengths and areas for improvement

My learning goals are to start to:

- understand the difference between evaluation and reflection in Global Perspectives
- identify and explain personal strengths
- identify areas for development

How will I know if I reach my goals?

As you work through this lesson and you achieve your learning goals, tick the 'Achieved' box to show you have completed this. If you haven't quite achieved your learning goals, tick 'Not there yet'. Start to think about how you are going to show your learning goals in your challenge. Add an example from your challenge once you have achieved each learning goal.

Lesson 1	Not there yet	Achieved	Example
I understand the difference between evaluation and reflection in Global Perspectives.			
I can identify and explain my personal strengths.			
I can identify areas I need to improve.			

Prior learning

1   What do you think the term 'evaluation' means in Global Perspectives lessons?

Evaluation is ....

....

2   What do you think the term 'reflection' means in Global Perspectives lessons?

Reflection is ....

....

3   Do you agree with your classmates about the meanings of evaluation and reflection in Global Perspectives lessons?   Yes/No

Why? ....

4   Using what you have learnt from class discussion, explain the difference between evaluation and reflection in Global Perspectives lessons in less than 20 words.

....

....

Starter activity

1 Which of these skills do you think you are good at?

A Listening to the ideas of others. ☐

B Asking for help. ☐

C Asking questions. ☐

D Giving an opinion. ☐

E Researching for evidence. ☐

F Identifying claims. ☐

G Giving reasoning for claims. ☐

H Summarising information in my own words. ☐

2 Why do you think you have these strengths?

....

....

3 Does your partner agree?

4 Which skills do you think need further development?

....

....

The topic I am working on today is …

....

Main activity

1 In a small group, discuss the text your teacher gives you and then answer the following questions.

a What is the text about?

....

> **Tip**
>
> Reflective learners encourage feedback and respond positively to praise and criticism.

> **Tip**
>
> Reflective learners think about how they are learning when completing learning activities; for example, they might learn best by discussing with others.

b What does each paragraph tell you?

Paragraph 1 (claim, reasoning, evidence): ....

....

....

Paragraph 2 (claim, reasoning, evidence): ....

....

....

Paragraph 3 (claim, reasoning, evidence): ....

....

....

Paragraph 4 (claim, reasoning, evidence): ....

....

....

2 Get into new groups. Share your information with your new group.

Did sharing help your learning to read and discuss the text with others?   Yes/No

Why? ....

....

....

> **Tip**
>
> Reflective learners can identify their personal strengths and explain these to others.

> **Tip**
>
> Reflective learners can identify any areas they need to develop, such as their listening or research skills.

> **Tip**
>
> Reflective learners can explain how they are going to improve or develop a skill; for example, improving reflective skills by asking themselves regularly how they learnt best.

Independent reflection activity

Which of these skills did you use or improve this lesson?

A   Listening to the ideas of others. ☐

B   Asking for help. ☐

C   Asking questions. ☐

D   Giving an opinion. ☐

E   Researching for evidence. ☐

F   Identifying claims. ☐

G   Giving reasoning for claims. ☐

H   Summarising information in own words. ☐

Which skills do you need to develop further?

....

....

....

How are you going to improve the skill(s) you have identified?

....

....

Check your learning

If you haven't already done so, complete the **How will I know if I reach my goals?** table with 'Not there yet' or 'Achieved'. Don't forget to add examples from your challenge.

Starting with reflection skills: Lesson 2

4.1 Explain personal contribution to teamwork and identify targets for improvement

4.2 Consider the benefits and challenges of teamwork experienced when working together to achieve a shared outcome

My learning goals are to start to:

- explain what teamwork is

- explain the benefits and challenges of teamwork

- explain personal contributions to teamwork

How will I know if I reach my goals?

As you work through this lesson and you achieve your learning goals, tick the 'Achieved' box to show you have completed this. If you haven't quite achieved your learning goals, tick 'Not there yet'. Start to think about how you are going to show your learning goals in your challenge. Add an example from your challenge once you have achieved each learning goal.

Lesson 2	Not there yet	Achieved	Example
I can explain what teamwork is.			
I can explain a benefit and a challenge of teamwork.			
I can explain my personal contribution to teamwork.			

Prior learning

1 Which of these abilities is the most important for teamwork? Discuss with a partner. Number them in order of importance, with 1 being the most important and 10 being the least important.

A   Listening to the ideas of others. ☐

B   Asking for help. ☐

C   Asking questions. ☐

D   Supporting and respecting each other. ☐

E   Taking turns to speak. ☐

F   Meeting deadlines. ☐

G   Knowing who is doing what. ☐

H   Keeping each other informed. ☐

I   Knowing when you are wrong. ☐

J   Being willing to take advice and criticism. ☐

2 Do your classmates agree with your order? Yes/No

3 Using what you've learnt from class discussion, make any changes to your order.

....

....

Starter activity

1   Using what you've learnt from class discussion in the Prior learning activity, complete these statements:

Teamwork is ....

....

Teamwork is not ....

....

2   Share your thinking with your classmates.
Do you agree with your classmates?   Yes/No

Why/Why not? ....

....

> **Tip**
>
> Effective teamwork relies on the combination of individual strengths brought to the team.

The topic I am working on today is …

....

Main activity

1   Look at the set of questions your teacher gives you.
    Discuss the questions and your answers with your team.

2   On a separate sheet of paper, produce a diagram, noting your team's
    responses to the questions. For example, you could use a mind map
    or a spider diagram.

3   Write down any other questions you could ask about the topic.
    Add your responses to your diagram.

        ....

        ....

        ....

Independent reflection activity

What contributions did you make to teamwork today?

....

What do you think are the benefits of teamwork?

....

What do you think are the challenges of teamwork?

....

> **Tip**
>
> Working *as* a team is different to working *in* a team. To work as a team, you need to work with a group of people to achieve a shared goal or outcome in an effective way.

> **Tip**
>
> It's important that each member of the team knows what they are doing to contribute to the team effort.

Check your learning

If you haven't already done so, complete the **How will I know if I reach my goals?** table with 'Not there yet' or 'Achieved'. Don't forget to add examples from your challenge.

Starting with reflection skills: Lesson 3

4.1 Explain personal contribution to teamwork and identify targets for improvement

4.2 Consider the benefits and challenges of teamwork experienced when working together to achieve a shared outcome

4.3 Consider ways that personal perspective on an issue may have changed as a result of conducting research or exploring different perspectives

---

My learning goals are to start to:

- explain the benefits and challenges of teamwork

- explain personal contributions to teamwork

- explain areas for improvement in teamwork

- explore personal perspective on a topic

How will I know if I reach my goals?

As you work through this lesson and you achieve your learning goals, tick the 'Achieved' box to show you have completed this. If you haven't quite achieved your learning goals, tick 'Not there yet'. Start to think about how you are going to show your learning goals in your challenge. Add an example from your challenge once you have achieved each learning goal.

Lesson 3	Not there yet	Achieved	Example
I can explain some benefits and challenges of teamwork.			
I can explain my contributions to teamwork.			
I can explain an area I can improve on in teamwork.			
I can reflect on my personal perspective about a topic.			

Prior learning

1   For each of the letters of the word 'teamwork', give a suitable word or phrase that helps explain what teamwork is. Discuss in your team.

T ....

E ....

A ....

M ....

W ....

O ....

R ....

K ....

2   Share your ideas with another team. Write down any better ideas from the other team.

....

....

The topic I am working on today is ...

....

Starter activity

For the Main activity in this lesson, your team will prepare and give a presentation to another team using your responses to the questions in the Main activity in Lesson 2.

Look back at your diagram from Lesson 2 and consider the personal abilities and strengths in your team. Who will have the following responsibilities in preparing the presentation?

A   Check that everyone is listening to each other. ....

B   Make sure that everyone is working to the time limit. ....

C   Make sure that all ideas are appreciated. ....

D   Check the clarity of the presentation, including spelling and grammar. ....

E   Make sure there is no conflict or that any conflict is resolved. ....

F   Encourage the team to work together. ....

G   Search for and suggest suitable images. ....

Main activity

1   Using the information gained from the Main activity in Lesson 2, plan a team presentation. The purpose of your presentation is to explain your team's views about the topic in Lesson 2 to another team in your class.

As a team, you need to present five slides. The first slide will show the title of your topic. Each of the other four slides will show an image and about four bullet points. The fifth slide will be the conclusion.

Tip

When reflecting on the benefits of teamwork, think about what you personally gain from working with a team.

Tip

When reflecting on the challenges of teamwork, think about what you and others might not like about working with a team.

Tip

A personal strength or quality is something that you are good at.

Tip

A limitation or weakness is usually something that is lacking or not done very well.

Plan each of your slides on a separate sheet of paper with:

- an image, or notes about it
- the bullet points for your slide
- notes to remind yourself what you want to say in the presentation.

Your plans for one slide might look like this:

Slide 2 ....

Image:

- ....

- ....

- ....

- ....

Notes ....

....

....

....

....

....

Tip

A personal perspective is the view that a person has on an issue after exploring different perspectives and reflecting on the causes and consequences of an issue.

Peer feedback

2 Give feedback on another team's presentation. Answer the following questions:

a Did the presentation have a suitable title?

b Was the content of the presentation clear?

c Did the images used make the presentation better?

d Was the content of the presentation interesting?

Tip

An area for development is something you need to improve on.

    e   Was the presentation delivered in an enthusiastic way?

    f   How might the presentation be improved?

....

....

Independent reflection activity

What were the benefits of working as a team this lesson?

....

....

What were the challenges of working as a team this lesson?

....

....

What was your actual contribution to teamwork this lesson?
How did this help towards the shared goal/outcome?

....

....

What do you need to improve on for the next teamwork activity? Why?

....

....

What is your personal perspective on the topic studied this lesson?

....

....

Check your learning

If you haven't already done so, complete the **How will I know if I reach my goals?** table with 'Not there yet' or 'Achieved'. Don't forget to add examples from your challenge.

Self-assessment 1

How much progress do you feel you have made so far in developing your reflection skills?

For each learning objective in the table below, shade in the response that matches yours most closely. Give one example for this response. Eventually, you are aiming for green!

Learning objectives: *to start to . . .*	RED	AMBER	GREEN
4.1 Explain personal contribution to teamwork and identify targets for improvement.	I can explain my contribution to teamwork with help. I can explain at least one target for improvement with help.	I can explain some of the ways I contribute to teamwork. I can explain at least one target for improvement.	I can explain some of the ways I contribute to teamwork and help others describe their contributions. I can explain some targets for improvement and help others identify targets for improvement.
4.2 Consider the benefits and challenges of teamwork experienced when working together to achieve a shared outcome.	I can explain at least one benefit and one challenge of teamwork with help.	I can explain some of the benefits and challenges of teamwork.	I can explain some of the benefits and challenges of teamwork and can help others explain the benefits or challenges of teamwork.
4.3 Consider ways that personal perspective on an issue may have changed as a result of conducting research or exploring different perspectives.	I can give my personal perspective on a topic with help.	I can give my personal perspective on a topic and say why I think like I do.	I can explain my personal perspective on a topic and help others explain their personal perspective on a topic.
4.4 Identify skills learnt or improved during an activity and relate to personal strengths and areas for improvement.	I can say what skills I have used or improved and say how I have used or improved them with help.	I can say what skills I have used or improved and say how I have used or improved them.	I can say what skills I have used or improved and say how I have used or improved them. I can help others explain what skills they have used or improved.

Continued

Examples:

4.1 ....

4.2 ....

4.3 ....

4.4 ....

Reflect on your responses in your self-assessment and identify two areas for improvement. Set yourself two learning targets – how you will improve upon the two areas. For example, 'I will try to appreciate all ideas even though we might not use them all in our shared outcome.'

Learning targets:

1 Area for improvement:

   How I will improve: ....

2 Area for improvement: ....

   How I will improve: ....

Challenge topic review

Think about the challenge topic you have been exploring and complete the statements.

I was surprised to discover that ....

I didn't know ....

I now think ....

Developing reflection skills: Lesson 4

4.1 Explain personal contribution to teamwork and identify targets for improvement

My learning goals are to develop my knowledge and understanding about:

- my contribution(s) to teamwork
- setting targets to improve my contribution(s) to teamwork

How will I know if I reach my goals?

As you work through this lesson and you achieve your learning goals, tick the 'Achieved' box to show you have completed this. If you haven't quite achieved your learning goals, tick 'Not there yet'. Start to think about how you are going to show your learning goals in your challenge. Add an example from your challenge once you have achieved each learning goal.

Lesson 4	Not there yet	Achieved	Example
I can explain my contribution(s) to teamwork.			
I can set at least one target to improve my contribution(s) to teamwork.			

Prior learning

1 Do you think working with others as a team presents more benefits or more challenges? Why?

I think ....

because ....

....

2 What does your partner think? Why?

My partner thinks ....

because ....

....

3 Using what you've learnt from class discussion about the benefits and challenges of teamwork, has your response to task **1** changed or not? Why?

....

....

....

The topic I am working on today is …

....

Starter activity

1 Working independently, write down all the words and phrases about the topic as you can in the time your teacher gives you.

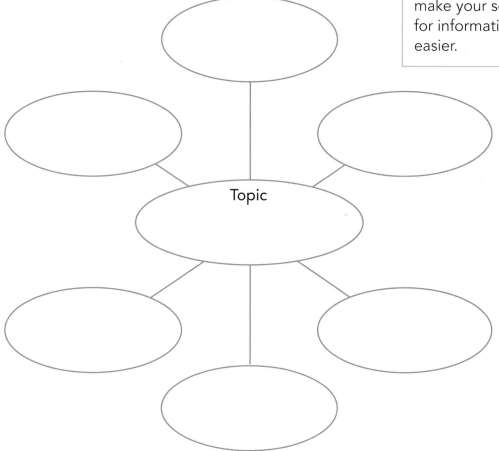

Topic

Peer feedback

2 After discussion with your partner, add to your diagram in a different colour.

Class discussion

3 After class discussion, add to your diagram in a different colour.

Main activity

1 Decide what research each member of your team is going to do to find out more about the topic.

2 Now that you have your research focus, complete the grid below.

	Name	Research focus	Websites/information sources
1			
2			
3			
4			
5			

a Make a brief note of different things you want to find out about in the table that follows. Then write one or two questions about each thing.

> **Tip**
>
> Questions that start with 'what', 'when', 'where' and 'who' are good questions for finding out facts.

b Do some research and find an answer to each question.

My research is about:			
My information sources/website addresses:			
	What I want to find out about	Questions	Answers
1			
2			
3			
4			
5			
6			

Tip

Tell someone else about what you've read. This will make sure you understand what you've read and that you can use your own words.

When making notes, ask yourself questions and put the answers from the information source in your own words.

Questions starting with 'why' and 'how' help you gain details to develop your understanding about an issue or a perspective.

Independent reflection activity

What contributions(s) did you make to teamwork this lesson?

....

What is/are your target(s) for improving your contribution(s) to teamwork?

....

Check your learning

If you haven't already done so, complete the **How will I know if I reach my goals?** table with 'Not there yet' or 'Achieved'. Don't forget to add examples from your challenge.

Developing reflection skills: Lesson 5

4.1 Explain personal contribution to teamwork and identify targets for improvement

4.4 Identify skills learnt or improved during an activity and relate to personal strengths and areas for improvement

My learning goals are to develop my knowledge and understanding about:

- contributing to teamwork
- how learning and improving skills adds to personal strengths

How will I know if I reach my goals?

As you work through this lesson and you achieve your learning goals, tick the 'Achieved' box to show you have completed this. If you haven't quite achieved your learning goals, tick 'Not there yet'. Start to think about how you are going to show your learning goals in your challenge. Add an example from your challenge once you have achieved each learning goal.

Lesson 5	Not there yet	Achieved	Example
I am increasing my contributions to teamwork.			
I can explain how I have learnt or improved a skill/skills.			
I understand that improving my skills adds to my personal strengths.			

Prior learning

With your team, consider your responses to the Independent reflection activity you did in Lesson 4.

1 What contributions(s) did you make to teamwork in Lesson 4?

....

2 What is/are your target(s) for improving your contribution(s) to teamwork?

....

3 Share your responses with your team. Do they agree?   Yes/No

4 Make any changes to your target(s) if need be.

....

....

The topic I am working on today is …

....

Starter activity

1 Look at the questions you wrote for task **2** in the Main activity in Lesson 4.

Which do you think are your best three questions?

1 ....

2 ....

3 ....

Peer feedback

2 Share your questions with a partner in your team.
Agree on your best three questions.

1 ....

2 ....

3 ....

3 Share your best three questions with your team. As a team, decide
on the best eight questions to give to another team to answer.

1 ....

2 ....

3 ....

4 ....

5 ....

6 ....

7 ....

8 ....

Tip

When researching
a topic, you
will often come
across interesting
information
that you can
use to develop
a perspective
or to explain
the causes and
consequences
of something, so
don't forget to
take notes.

Main activity

1 a Working as a team, use this grid to record
the questions another team has given you.

   b Individually or in pairs, do some research
to discover the answers.

c   Then fill in the answers as a team.

	Research topic:	
	From team:	
	Questions	**Answers**
1		
2		
3		
4		
5		
6		
7		
8		

2 Record any further interesting information you find out about the topic.

....

....

....

....

....

....

Tip

Always take notes about any information that influences your own opinion about a topic. You will find this useful when reflecting on your personal perspective.

Independent reflection activity

What skill have you used or improved today?

....

Do you think this skill is now becoming a personal strength?

Yes/No

Why?..

Did you improve your contributions(s) to teamwork this lesson?

Yes/No

How? ....

Why not?..

Check your learning

If you haven't already done so, complete the **How will I know if I reach my goals?** table with 'Not there yet' or 'Achieved'. Don't forget to add examples from your challenge.

Developing reflection skills: Lesson 6

4.2 Consider the benefits and challenges of teamwork experienced when working together to achieve a shared outcome

4.3 Consider ways that personal perspective on an issue may have changed as a result of conducting research or exploring different perspectives

---

My learning goals are to develop my knowledge and understanding about:

- the challenges of teamwork and how to overcome these

- how a personal perspective can develop or change after research and considering different perspectives

---

How will I know if I reach my goals?

As you work through this lesson and you achieve your learning goals, tick the 'Achieved' box to show you have completed this. If you haven't quite achieved your learning goals, tick 'Not there yet'. Start to think about how you are going to show your learning goals in your challenge. Add an example from your challenge once you have achieved each learning goal.

Lesson 6	Not there yet	Achieved	Example
I can explain some of the challenges of teamwork.			
I can explain how to overcome some of the challenges of teamwork.			
I can explain how my personal perspective about a topic has developed or changed.			

Prior learning

1   Discuss the following questions with a partner.

   a   What do you think the term 'personal perspective' means in Global Perspectives?

   ....

   b   How do you think a personal perspective differs from a global or national perspective?

   ....

   ....

2   Using what you learn from class discussion, make any changes to your responses in task **1** in a different colour.

Tip

The ideas and experiences of others all influence your own personal perspective.

Tip

You can change your personal perspective as a result of research and exploring different perspectives on a topic or issue.

The topic I am working on today is …

....

Starter activity

Look back at how you worked as a team in Lesson 5.
On your own, answer the following questions as honestly as you can:

1   Do you feel that you contributed enough to the teamwork in the Starter activity in Lesson 5? Yes/No

   a   How did you contribute? ....

   b   If you did not contribute enough, why not? ....

   ....

2   Do you feel that you contributed enough to the teamwork in the Main activity in Lesson 5?   Yes/No

   a   How did you contribute? ....

   b   If you did not contribute enough, why not? ....

3 **a** What challenges did you face as a team in the Starter activity in Lesson 5? ....

....

b How did you overcome these challenges? ....

....

4 **a** What challenges did you face as a team in the Main activity in Lesson 5? ....

....

b How did you overcome these challenges? ....

....

> **Tip**
>
> A national perspective is the view that a particular country has on an issue. This is usually explained by the laws, policies and/or speeches made by politicians of that country and might be supported by other groups within that country.

Main activity

1 Look back at the information you gained on your topic from the Main activity in Lesson 5. Using a separate sheet of paper, work as a team to create a poster to present the information to your classmates.

Peer feedback

2 As a team, give feedback to each of the other teams for their poster. Write one highlight and one area for improvement for each team on sticky notes like the ones below.

> **Tip**
>
> A global perspective is a view on an issue that either has global influence or takes account of the nature of the issue globally.

Team: *3*

Highlight: *Includes some facts as evidence*

Improvement: *What is the perspective?*

Team:

Highlight:

Improvement:

Team:

Highlight:

Improvement:

Independent reflection activity

Reflect on your learning from viewing the posters in the Main activity.
Answer the following questions:

Did you learn anything new this lesson? If so, what?

....

....

What did you think about the topic before you started working on it?

....

Has your personal perspective about the topic changed?　　　　Yes/No

How? ....

....

....

Is your personal perspective about the topic the same but stronger?　　Yes/No

Why?..

Check your learning

If you haven't already done so, complete the **How will I know if I reach my goals?** table with 'Not there yet' or 'Achieved'. Don't forget to add examples from your challenge.

Self-assessment 2

Look back at self-assessment 1. How much further progress do you feel you have made so far in developing your reflection skills?

For each learning objective in the table that follows, shade in the response that matches yours most closely. Give one example for this response. Eventually, you are aiming for green!

Continued

Learning objectives: *to develop my knowledge and understanding about how to . . .*	RED	AMBER	GREEN
4.1 Explain personal contribution to teamwork and identify targets for improvement.	I can explain at least one way I contribute to teamwork. I can explain at least one target for improvement.	I can explain some of the ways I contribute to teamwork. I can explain some targets for improvement.	I can explain some of the ways I can contribute to teamwork and help others describe their contributions to teamwork. I can explain targets for improvement and help others explain targets for improvement.
4.2 Consider the benefits and challenges of teamwork experienced when working together to achieve a shared outcome.	I can explain at least one benefit and one challenge of teamwork but may need help to do so.	I can explain some of the benefits and challenges of teamwork. I can describe ways of overcoming challenges with help.	I can explain some of the benefits and challenges of teamwork. I can describe ways of overcoming challenges. I can help others explain the benefits and challenges of teamwork.
4.3 Consider ways that personal perspective on an issue may have changed as a result of conducting research or exploring different perspectives.	I understand what a personal perspective is. I can give my personal perspective and support this with some evidence with help.	I understand the difference between a personal, a global and a national perspective. I can give my personal perspective and support this with some evidence.	I understand the difference between a personal, a global and a national perspective. I can give my personal perspective and support this with evidence. I can help others determine their personal perspective on a topic.

Continued

Learning objectives: *how to develop my knowledge and understanding about how to . . .*	RED	AMBER	GREEN
4.4 Identify skills learnt or improved during an activity and relate to personal strengths and areas for improvement.	I can explain at least one skill I have used or improved during an activity with help. I can say how I have used or improved it with help.	I can explain which skill(s) I have used or improved during an activity. I can explain how I have used or improved it/them. I can identify at least one skill that needs improvement.	I can explain the skills I have used or improved during learning activities. I can explain how I have used or improved them. I can identify a skill that needs improvement and explain how I will improve this skill. I can help others identify a skill they need to improve.

Examples:

4.1 ....

4.2 ....

4.3 ....

4.4 ....

Continued

Reflect on your responses in your self-assessment and identify two areas for improvement. Set yourself two learning targets – how you will improve upon the two areas. For example, 'I will make sure that I support my personal perspective with some evidence.'

Learning targets:

1 Area for improvement: ....

   How I will improve: ....

2 Area for improvement: ....

   How I will improve: ....

Challenge topic review

Think about the challenge topic you have been exploring and complete the following statements.

I was surprised to discover that ....

I didn't know ....

I now think ....

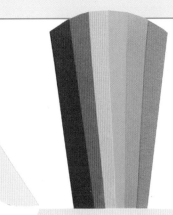

7

Getting better at reflection skills: Lesson 7

4.1 Explain personal contribution to teamwork and identify targets for improvement

4.4 Identify skills learnt or improved during an activity and relate to personal strengths and areas for improvement

My learning goals are to get better at:

- understanding that my personal strengths can benefit teamwork

- working with others towards a shared outcome

- explaining skills used and improved

How will I know if I reach my goals?

As you work through this lesson and you achieve your learning goals, tick the 'Achieved' box to show you have completed this. If you haven't quite achieved your learning goals, tick 'Not there yet'. Start to think about how you are going to show your learning goals in your challenge. Add an example from your challenge once you have achieved each learning goal.

Lesson 7	Not there yet	Achieved	Example
I understand how some of my personal strengths can benefit teamwork.			
I can work with others towards a shared outcome.			
I can explain the skills I have used or improved.			

Prior learning

1 Which of these do you think are your personal strengths?

	Personal strengths	Yes	No
A	I know how to do effective research using a search engine.		
B	I know the difference between evaluation and reflection in Global Perspectives.		
C	I know that I need to support my personal perspective with evidence.		
D	I am good at thinking of courses of actions for issues.		
E	I am good at listening to the ideas of others.		
F	I am good at saying what I think.		

2 As a class, share examples for the strengths ticked 'Yes'.

....

....

3 Reflecting on the class discussion, what other personal strengths do you have?

....

4 Share examples of your other personal strengths with your team.

....

5 Why do you think your personal strengths can be of benefit to teamwork?

....

The topic I am working on today is …

....

Starter activity

1   Look at the picture your teacher shows you.
    What is the issue in the picture?

    ....

2   What do you know about the issue?

    ....

    ....

    ....

3   What do you need to consider before suggesting a course of
    action to try to help resolve the issue?

    ....

    ....

    ....

    ....

Main activity

1   Work in teams. Consider the issue from the Starter activity and
    write it as a question.

    ....

> **Tip**
>
> It's always a good idea for each team member to do some of the research as well as having another role in producing the shared outcome.

> **Tip**
>
> When thinking about courses of action, consider how they will work to help resolve the issue or make a positive difference to an issue.

> **Tip**
>
> Try not to think too big. Think of a course of action you and your classmates can take, such as creating a presentation to raise awareness about an issue to make people think differently.

2 Complete the table to decide on a possible course of action.

Issue (as a question):		
Possible course of action	Reasons for/against choosing this action	Other considerations about this action (e.g. What resources are needed?)
1		
2		
3		

Independent reflection activity

What skill(s) have you used today? ....

....

How? ....

What skill do you still need to improve? ....

Why? ....

Check your learning

If you haven't already done so, complete the **How will I know if I reach my goals?** table with 'Not there yet' or 'Achieved'. Don't forget to add examples from your challenge.

Getting better at reflection skills: Lesson 8

4.1 Explain personal contribution to teamwork and identify targets for improvement

4.4 Identify skills learnt or improved during an activity and relate to personal strengths and areas for improvement

My learning goals are to get better at:

- explaining my personal contribution(s) to teamwork
- explaining the skills that I have learnt or improved
- explaining areas for improvement

How will I know if I reach my goals?

As you work through this lesson and you achieve your learning goals, tick the 'Achieved' box to show you have completed this. If you haven't quite achieved your learning goals, tick 'Not there yet'. Start to think about how you are going to show your learning goals in your challenge. Add an example from your challenge once you have achieved each learning goal.

Lesson 8	Not there yet	Achieved	Example
I can explain my personal contribution(s) to teamwork.			
I can explain the skills that I have learned or improved.			
I can explain an area I need to work on or improve.			

Prior learning

1   In teams, discuss what the term 'course of action' means in Global Perspectives.

....

....

2   What do you need to consider when suggesting a course of action?

- ....

- ....

- ....

- ....

- ....

The topic I am working on today is ...

....

Starter activity

Look at the course of action you decided on in Lesson 7.
Answer the questions.

1   Is the course of action specific to the issue?   Yes/No

    because ....

2   Is it measurable?   Yes/No

    because ....

3   Is it achievable?   Yes/No

    because ....

4   Is it realistic?   Yes/No

    because ....

5   Can you do it in the time allowed?   Yes/No

    because ....

Tip

Questions to test if a course of action is **specific** include 'Does it relate to the issue?' and 'What exactly are we trying to achieve?'

A question to test if a course of action is **measurable** is 'How will we know if it's successful?'

Questions to test if a course of action is **achievable** include 'Can we do it within the given time?' and 'Can we do it with the resources we have?'

A question to test if a course of action is **realistic** is 'Is it practical?'

A question to test if a course of action is **time-bound** is 'Do we have enough time?'

Main activity

1   Use this grid to record your team action plan to create your team outcome.

Tip

When planning, each member of a team needs a specific job as well as taking part in the research.

Issue	
Course of action	
Team outcome	
Team members	

Start date	Completion date	Task (What?) Action (How?)	Person responsible	Resources needed

Tip

Taking time at the beginning of a team project to allocate roles and responsibilities to team members according to their personal strengths is time well spent and will support more effective teamwork.

2   On a separate piece of paper, complete your team outcome.

Peer feedback

3 Give and receive feedback on the team outcomes. What did your peers say about your team outcome? Answer the questions.

a Is it related to the issue?   Yes/No

b Can it help towards resolving the issue?   Yes/No

c Can it make a positive difference to the issue?   Yes/No

d Are the key messages clear?   Yes/No

e Does it include different perspectives?   Yes/No

f Is it a realistic course of action?   Yes/No

g Any other feedback?

....

....

....

> **Tip**
>
> Local research will involve talking with people who are experts in their field, such as teachers in school or parents who work for a specific company.

> **Tip**
>
> Allocate tasks according to the personal strengths of team members.

Independent reflection activity

How did you contribute to teamwork today?

....

What skill did you learn today?

....

What skill do you still need to improve?

....

How are you going to improve it?

....

Check your learning

If you haven't already done so, complete the **How will I know if I reach my goals?** table with 'Not there yet' or 'Achieved'. Don't forget to add examples from your challenge.

9

Getting better at reflection skills: Lesson 9

4.2 Consider the benefits and challenges of teamwork experienced when working together to achieve a shared outcome

4.3 Consider ways that personal perspective on an issue may have changed as a result of conducting research or exploring different perspectives

My learning goals are to get better at:

- explaining the challenges of teamwork

- explaining how to overcome the challenges of teamwork

- explaining my personal perspective on an issue

How will I know if I reach my goals?

As you work through this lesson and you achieve your learning goals, tick the 'Achieved' box to show you have completed this. If you haven't quite achieved your learning goals, tick 'Not there yet'. Start to think about how you are going to show your learning goals in your challenge. Add an example from your challenge once you have achieved each learning goal.

Lesson 9	Not there yet	Achieved	Example
I can explain some of the challenges of teamwork.			
I can explain how to overcome some of the challenges of teamwork.			
I can explain my personal perspective.			

Prior learning

1   In teams, discuss the challenges of teamwork.
    Choose one challenge your team has faced.

    ....

2   What did you do to overcome this challenge?

    ....

3   How else might you overcome this challenge?

    ....

The topic I am working on today is …

....

Starter activity

Discuss the following questions with your team:

1   What feedback was given in Lesson 8 about your team outcome?

    • ....

    • ....

    • ....

    • ....

2   What changes do you need to make to improve your team outcome?

    ....

    ....

Tip

When evaluating an outcome, as well as considering the limitations and areas for improvement, also reflect on the highlights.

Tip

As well as asking your peers to evaluate your team outcome, ask the audience for whom you created the team outcome.

Main activity

1 Complete your team outcome, making the changes you have identified.

2 Use this grid to evaluate your team outcome from the point of view of the target audience.

Tip

Work in your team to evaluate your team outcome as different members of the team will think different things.

	Evaluating team outcome	Yes	No	Action
1	Is your outcome related to the issue?			
2	Do you think it can help towards resolving the issue?			
3	Do you think it can make a positive difference to the issue?			
4	Do you understand the key messages in your outcome?			
5	Does it include different perspectives?			
6	Is it a realistic course of action?			
7	Other evaluation questions?			

Tip

Always try to give a reason and evidence to support your personal perspective.
Say: 'I think this, because . . .'

Independent reflection activity

Complete the following statements:

Before completing this section on reflection skills, I thought reflection was ....

....

....

Now, I think ....

....

This is due to ....

....

How has your personal perspective about the issue in Lessons 7–9 developed
or changed?

....

....

Check your learning

If you haven't already done so, complete the **How will I know if I reach my goals?** table
with 'Not there yet' or 'Achieved'. Don't forget to add examples from your challenge.

Self-assessment 3

Look back at self-assessments 1 and 2. How much further progress do you feel you have made so far in developing your reflection skills?

For each learning objective in the table below, shade in the response that matches yours most closely. Give one example for this response. Eventually, you are aiming for green!

Learning objectives: *to get better at understanding how to . . .*	RED	AMBER	GREEN
4.1 Explain personal contribution to teamwork and identify targets for improvement.	I can explain how I contribute to teamwork, referring to my personal strengths. I can explain some targets for improvement with help.	I can explain how I contribute to teamwork, referring to my personal strengths. I can explain some targets for improvement.	I can explain how I contribute to teamwork, referring to my personal strengths. I can explain some targets for improvement. I can help others explain how their personal strengths can contribute to teamwork and help them explain targets for improvement.
4.2 Consider the benefits and challenges of teamwork experienced when working together to achieve a shared outcome.	I can explain some of the benefits and challenges of teamwork. I can suggest ways of addressing some challenges with help.	I can explain some of the benefits and challenges of teamwork. I can suggest ways of addressing some challenges.	I can explain some of the benefits and challenges of teamwork. I can suggest ways of addressing some challenges and advise others about how to overcome some of the challenges.

Continued

Learning objectives: *to get better at understanding how to . . .*	RED	AMBER	GREEN
4.3 Consider ways that personal perspective on an issue may have changed as a result of conducting research or exploring different perspectives.	I understand what a personal perspective is. I can say if my personal perspective has developed or changed, and support this with some evidence with help.	I understand what a personal perspective is. I can explain if my personal perspective has developed or changed, and support this with evidence.	I understand what a personal perspective is. I can explain if my personal perspective has developed or changed, and support this with evidence. I can help others explain how their personal perspective on an issue may have changed.
4.4 Identify skills learnt or improved during an activity and relate to personal strengths and areas for improvement.	I can explain a skill I have used or improved during an activity. I can say how I have used or improved it. I can identify a skill I still need to improve with help.	I can explain the skills I have used or improved during an activity. I can explain how I have used or improved them. I can identify a skill I still need to improve and say how I am going to improve it.	I can explain the skills I have used or improved during an activity. I can explain how I have used or improved them. I can explain how I am going to improve a skill and give help to others to improve their skills.

Examples:

4.1 ....

4.2 ....

4.3 ....

4.4 ....

Continued

Reflect on your responses in your self-assessment and identify two areas for improvement. Set yourself two learning targets – how you will improve upon the two areas. For example, 'I will try to help my partner identify a skill they need to improve and suggest ways that they can do this.'

Learning targets:

1 Area for improvement: ....

How I will improve: ....

2 Area for improvement: ....

How I will improve: ....

Challenge topic review

Think about the challenge topic you have been exploring and complete the following statements.

I was surprised to discover that ....

I didn't know ....

I now think ....

Collaboration

This section of your Learner's Skills Book 8 helps you to develop your collaboration skills using interesting global topics.

Starting with . . .

As you start to develop your collaboration skills in Stage 8, you will be learning what we mean by collaborating in Global Perspectives lessons. You will explore some of the characteristics that team members might have and how these help with effective collaboration. As well as collaboration skills, you will continue to develop the other Global Perspectives skills as you explore ideas and evidence from different perspectives within different information sources.

Developing . . .

As you further develop your collaboration skills in Stage 8, you will be working in teams and developing your understanding about how to resolve any conflicts during teamwork. You will use the ideas and information you have gained from research and from team members to create a shared outcome with your team.

Getting better at . . .

As you get better at collaboration in Stage 8, not only will you be continuing to work in teams to produce shared outcomes, you will also be exploring how to give and receive feedback from others about work you and/or they have produced. You will reflect on and evaluate the effectiveness of the team and your own role during teamwork.

Starting with collaboration skills: Lesson 1

5.1 The team assign roles and divide tasks fairly, considering the skills of team members and time available, and work together to achieve a shared outcome

5.2 The team member introduces useful ideas to help achieve a shared outcome and works positively to resolve conflict, solve issues and encourage other team members to participate, when required

My learning goals are to start to:

- explain the term 'collaboration'
- explain how to collaborate in Global Perspectives lessons
- explain the characteristics that team members need for effective collaboration

How will I know if I reach my goals?

As you work through this lesson and you achieve your learning goals, tick the 'Achieved' box to show you have completed this. If you haven't quite achieved your learning goals, tick 'Not there yet'. Start to think about how you are going to show your learning goals in your challenge. Add an example from your challenge once you have achieved each learning goal.

Lesson 1	Not there yet	Achieved	Example
I know what collaboration is.			
I can explain how I collaborate in Global Perspectives lessons.			
I can explain some of the characteristics team members need for effective collaboration.			

Prior learning

1   Discuss with a partner. What does the term 'collaboration' mean to you?

    ....

2   Give some examples of how you collaborate in Global Perspectives lessons.

    ....

    ....

    ....

3   Using what you have learnt from class discussion, add further examples of collaboration.

    ....

    ....

Starter activity

1   Someone you know is organising a charity event. Which of these characteristics would you advise them to look for when picking their team to help organise this event? Discuss with a partner.

A   Shares good ideas. ☐

B   Likes talking. ☐

C   Likes listening to others. ☐

D   Likes giving their opinion. ☐

E   Likes to be in charge. ☐

F   Complains all the time. ☐

G   Often disappears. ☐

H   Follows instructions. ☐

I   Is organised. ☐

J   Is argumentative. ☐

K   Doesn't like working with others. ☐

L   Is good at drawing. ☐

2   Explain why you have picked these characteristics.

....

....

....

3   Do your classmates agree?   Yes/No

Why? ....

4   After discussion with your partner, which three of the characteristics do you think are the most important? Why?

....

....

....

> **Tip**
>
> A claim is a statement or assertion that something is true, typically without providing supporting evidence or proof and answers the question 'What do I think?'

> **Tip**
>
> Claims need justifying with reasoning so always look for reasons why someone states something. A reason answers the question 'Why do I think this?'

The topic I am working on today is …

....

Main activity

1 Read the text your teacher shows you.

   a What is the text about?

   ....

   b Give one claim in the text.

   ....

   c What reasoning in the text justifies this claim?

   ....

   d What evidence in the text supports this claim?

   ....

   e Do you think the text contains bias? Why?

   ....

Peer feedback

2 Discuss what you have found out with your team. Add any further ideas to your responses to **a–e** in a different colour.

3 Discuss the question your teacher gives you. Complete the table as a team.

> **Tip**
>
> You need to give evidence to support a claim. Evidence comes from research and answers the question 'How do I know this?'

> **Tip**
>
> Bias is a judgment based on a personal point of view. People who are biased often believe what they want to believe, refusing to take different perspectives or the opinions of others into consideration.

K What we **K**now	• .... • .... • ....
W What we **W**onder about	• .... • .... • ....
H **H**ow we are going to find out about what we wonder about	• .... • .... • ....

Independent reflection activity

Do you think you participated in teamwork this lesson?   Yes/No

Why?..

How could you improve your participation in teamwork?

....

Check your learning

If you haven't already done so, complete the **How will I know if I reach my goals?** table with 'Not there yet' or 'Achieved'. Don't forget to add examples from your challenge.

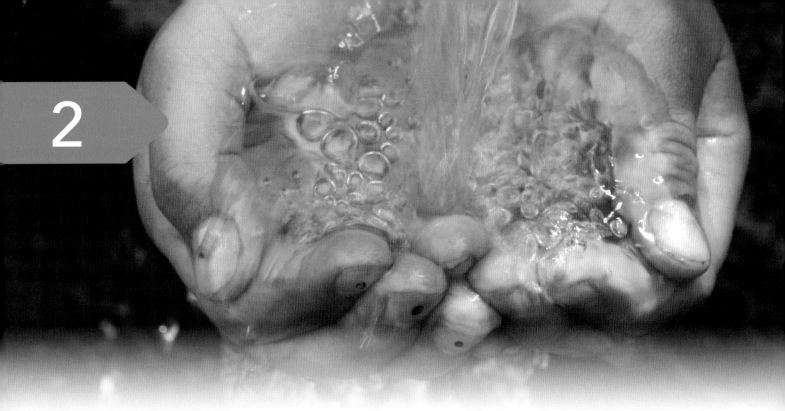

2

Starting with collaboration skills: Lesson 2

5.1 The team assign roles and divide tasks fairly, considering the skills of team members and time available, and work together to achieve a shared outcome

5.2 The team member introduces useful ideas to help achieve a shared outcome and works positively to resolve conflict, solve issues and encourage other team members to participate, when required

My learning goals are to start to:

- explain the strengths of individual team members

- share relevant ideas with team members

- work with a team to plan and produce a shared outcome

How will I know if I reach my goals?

As you work through this lesson and you achieve your learning goals, tick the 'Achieved' box to show you have completed this. If you haven't quite achieved your learning goals, tick 'Not there yet'. Start to think about how you are going to show your learning goals in your challenge. Add an example from your challenge once you have achieved each learning goal.

Lesson 2	Not there yet	Achieved	Example
I can explain some of the strengths my team members possess.			
I can share some relevant ideas with my team members.			
I can work with a team to plan and produce a shared outcome.			

Prior learning

1 Who is good at what? Write your team members' names against the appropriate strengths.

Strength	Team member(s)
Good at . . .	
sharing ideas	
organising	
listening to others	
giving their opinion	
taking charge	
being creative	
following instructions	
meeting deadlines	
presenting ideas	
motivating others	

Did you all agree?   Yes/No

2 How did you overcome any disagreements?

....

The topic I am working on today is …

....

Starter activity

Look at the question your teacher shows you. Discuss it with a partner. What words/phrases are going to be useful to prepare a response to this question?

....

....

....

....

Tip

When working out what strengths you have, think about what you do well and like doing.

Tip

Each member of a team should be aware of the personal strengths they bring to the team.

Tip

For effective collaboration, all team members must try to compromise and come to an agreement.

Main activity

1   Your team is going to create a visual presentation on this topic, based on the question you have been discussing. Discuss your team perspective and the arguments you will use in your presentation, using this grid to record your thinking. You may need to do some research.

Our question: ....
Our perspective:
Arguments
1   Source of information: Notes:

Arguments	
2 Source of information: Notes:	
3 Source of information: Notes:	
4 Source of information: Notes:	
5 Source of information: Notes:	

2 Now create your visual presentation, using the following checklist:

Team:		
Question:		
Check that you have . . .	YES (✓)	Notes
a range of visuals (text, images)		
text font and size of text suitable for the audience		

Check that you have . . .	YES (✓)	Notes
a clear structure (beginning, middle and end)		
content that is relevant		
content that answers the question		
claims that are supported with reasoning and evidence		
contributions from everyone in the team		

Independent reflection activity

What strengths did you bring to the team?

....

What areas do you need to improve on to be a more effective member of a team?

....

Check your learning

If you haven't already done so, complete the **How will I know if I reach my goals?** table with 'Not there yet' or 'Achieved'. Don't forget to add examples from your challenge.

3

Starting with collaboration skills: Lesson 3

5.1 The team assign roles and divide tasks fairly, considering the skills of team members and time available, and work together to achieve a shared outcome

5.2 The team member introduces useful ideas to help achieve a shared outcome and works positively to resolve conflict, solve issues and encourage other team members to participate, when required

My learning goals are to start to:

- explain the strengths of individual team members
- work with a team to review and evaluate a shared outcome

How will I know if I reach my goals?

As you work through this lesson and you achieve your learning goals, tick the 'Achieved' box to show you have completed this. If you haven't quite achieved your learning goals, tick 'Not there yet'. Start to think about how you are going to show your learning goals in your challenge. Add an example from your challenge once you have achieved each learning goal.

Lesson 3	Not there yet	Achieved	Example
I can explain some of the strengths my team members possess.			
I can work with a team to review and evaluate a shared outcome.			

Prior learning

1 Which of these factors is the most and least important when presenting an argument? Discuss them with a partner and then rank the other factors between.

A The pictures are large.

B I sound as if I know what I am talking about.

C The content is clear.

D There are no pictures.

E I justify my claims with reasoning.

F There are lots of words on each slide.

G I speak slowly.

H I speak quickly.

I I maintain eye contact with the audience.

J I use my arms when speaking.

K I support my claims with evidence.

1 Most ....

2 ....

3 ....

4 ....

5 ....

6 ....

7 ....

8 ....

9 ....

10 Least ....

Do your classmates agree?   Yes/No

Continued

2 After class discussion, which three do you think are the most important?

1 ....

2 ....

3 ....

The topic I am working on today is …

....

Starter activity

With your team, review the presentation you created in Lesson 2. What improvements need making?

1 ....

....

....

2 ....

....

....

3 ....

....

....

> **Tip**
>
> A shared outcome is something you produce with a team, such as a presentation, poster or video clip.

> **Tip**
>
> When making a presentation, body language and being clear are just as important as what you say.

> **Tip**
>
> When presenting a shared outcome, every member of the team should participate.

Main activity

Use this grid to record your responses as you listen to another team's presentation.

Team:		
Question:		
	Opinion	Comment
Was there a range of visuals (text, images)?	🙂 🙂 😐	
Was the type of font and size suitable for the audience?	🙂 🙂 😐	
Was there a clear structure (beginning, middle and end)?	🙂 🙂 😐	
Was the content relevant?	🙂 🙂 😐	
Did the content answer the question?	🙂 🙂 😐	
Were the arguments supported with evidence?	🙂 🙂 😐	
Did the presenters make eye contact with the audience?	🙂 🙂 😐	
Did they speak clearly?	🙂 🙂 😐	
Were all members of the team actively involved?	🙂 🙂 😐	

Peer feedback comments:

Highlight(s):

Area(s) for development:

Teacher feedback comments:

Self-assessment comments:

Targets for development:

1

2

3

Independent reflection activity

List the skills and strengths your team used this lesson.

Team member	Skill	Example

What skills do you think team members still need to work on?

Team member	Skill

Check your learning

If you haven't already done so, complete the **How will I know if I reach my goals?** table with 'Not there yet' or 'Achieved'. Don't forget to add examples from your challenge.

Self-assessment 1

How much progress do you feel you have made so far in developing your collaboration skills?

For each learning objective in the table below, shade in the response that matches yours most closely. Give one example for this response. Eventually, you are aiming for green!

Learning objectives: *to start to understand how …*	RED	AMBER	GREEN
5.1 The team assign roles and divide tasks fairly, considering the skills of team members and time available, and work together to achieve a shared outcome.	I understand what the term 'collaboration' means in Global Perspectives, and I can give examples with help. I can give examples for some of my strengths and some of my teammates' strengths with help.	I understand what the term 'collaboration' means in Global Perspectives and I can give examples. I can give examples for some of my strengths and some of my teammates' strengths. I can explain some ways of developing my collaboration skills with help.	I understand what the term 'collaboration' means in Global Perspectives and I can give examples. I can explain the importance of some of my strengths and skills for effective teamwork. I can explain the importance of some of my teammates' strengths and skills for effective teamwork. I can suggest ways of developing collaboration skills.
5.2 The team member introduces useful ideas to help achieve a shared outcome and works positively to resolve conflict, solve issues and encourage other team members to participate, when required.	I can share some relevant ideas with others. I can explain how some of my contributions help towards planning and producing a shared outcome with help.	I can share relevant ideas with others. I can explain how my contributions help towards planning and producing a shared outcome. With help, I can encourage team members to participate.	I can share relevant ideas with others. I can explain how all team members' contributions help towards planning and producing a shared outcome. I can encourage team members to participate and help to resolve any conflict.

Continued

Examples:

5.1 ....

5.2 ....

Reflect on your responses in your self-assessment and identify two areas for improvement. Set yourself two learning targets – how you will improve upon the two areas. For example, 'I could be more organised so that the team members all know what they are doing and when by.'

Learning targets:

1   Area for improvement: ....

   How I will improve: ....

2   Area for improvement: ....

   How I will improve: ....

Challenge topic review

Think about the challenge topic you have been exploring and complete the following statements.

I was surprised to discover that ....

I didn't know ....

I now think ....

Developing collaboration skills: Lesson 4

5.1 The team assign roles and divide tasks fairly, considering the skills of team members and time available, and work together to achieve a shared outcome

5.2 The team member introduces useful ideas to help achieve a shared outcome and works positively to resolve conflict, solve issues and encourage other team members to participate, when required

My learning goals are to develop my knowledge and understanding about:

- resolving conflict during teamwork
- collaboration to achieve shared outcomes

How will I know if I reach my goals?

As you work through this lesson and you achieve your learning goals, tick the 'Achieved' box to show you have completed this. If you haven't quite achieved your learning goals, tick 'Not there yet'. Start to think about how you are going to show your learning goals in your challenge. Add an example from your challenge once you have achieved each learning goal.

Lesson 4	Not there yet	Achieved	Example
I can help resolve conflict during teamwork.			
I can work with others towards a common goal.			

Prior learning

1 What was the most important thing you learnt about collaboration last lesson?

....

2 How are you going to improve your collaboration skills this lesson?

....

3 Share your ideas with your team. Record their responses.

Name	How to improve collaboration skills	Y/N	Action
Me			

The topic I am working on today is ...

....

Starter activity

1   Look at the questions your teacher shows you.
    Write down your thoughts in answer to each of the questions.

    Question 1: ....

    ....

    Question 2: ....

    ....

    Question 3: ....

    ....

    Question 4: ....

    ....

    Question 5: ....

    ....

    Question 6: ....

    ....

Class discussion

2   Using what you've learnt from class discussion, add further ideas in a different colour.

Main activity

1 Consider the scenario your teacher gives you. In pairs, write down five interview questions you could ask. You may need to do some research to decide on your questions.

Topic:
Interview questions
1
2
3
4
5

Tip

Having the rule that everyone's ideas are valid and won't be ignored, even if team members don't agree with them, helps avoid conflict.

Tip

Agree to compromise. Most of the time, individual points can be combined to make a better idea or solution.

2 Discuss the questions in your team, then write down the five best interview questions.

Topic:
Interview questions
1
2
3
4
5

Tip

Part of teamwork is being able to see another point of view, even if you don't agree with it at first.

3 Discuss the questions in class, then write down the five best interview questions.

Topic:
Interview questions
1
2
3
4
5

Tip

To develop a local perspective, you will need to gain information from local people. This can include your family, friends, staff at your school and, in your community centre, shopkeepers, restaurant owners, etc.

Independent reflection activity

Did you achieve your goal for developing your collaboration skills this lesson?   Yes/No

How? ....

What conflict was there during teamwork this lesson?

....

How was this conflict resolved?

....

....

Did you and your teammates improve your collaboration skills this lesson.
Complete the table in your prior learning.

Check your learning

If you haven't already done so, complete the **How will I know if I reach my goals?** table with 'Not there yet' or 'Achieved'. Don't forget to add examples from your challenge.

5

Developing collaboration skills: Lesson 5

5.1 The team assign roles and divide tasks fairly, considering the skills of team members and time available, and work together to achieve a shared outcome

5.2 The team member introduces useful ideas to help achieve a shared outcome and works positively to resolve conflict, solve issues and encourage other team members to participate, when required

My learning goals are to develop my knowledge and understanding about:

- collaborating to produce shared outcomes
- contributing ideas to shared outcomes

How will I know if I reach my goals?

As you work through this lesson and you achieve your learning goals, tick the 'Achieved' box to show you have completed this. If you haven't quite achieved your learning goals, tick 'Not there yet'. Start to think about how you are going to show your learning goals in your challenge. Add an example from your challenge once you have achieved each learning goal.

Lesson 5	Not there yet	Achieved	Example
I can work with others towards a common goal.			
I can share relevant ideas to produce a shared outcome.			

Prior learning

1   Discuss the following statements with a partner. Then complete them.

   a   A shared outcome in Global Perspectives is:

   ....

   b   An example of a shared outcome in Global Perspectives is:

   ....

2   Discuss your ideas with your classmates. Add further ideas in a different colour.

The topic I am working on today is …

....

Starter activity

In your team, review the information gained from your interview questions in Lesson 4.

1 What did you find out?

....

....

2 What further information do you need?

....

....

3 How are you going to find this out?

....

....

4 What shared outcome are you going to create?

....

....

5 Why have you chosen this outcome?

....

6 Who is going to do what?

....

....

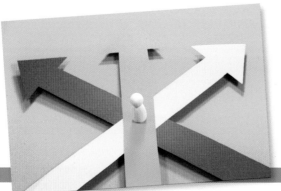

> **Tip**
>
> Collaborating to produce a shared outcome allows all team members to use their personal strengths, think creatively and share their ideas.

> **Tip**
>
> An aim is the purpose of the shared outcome. You can answer the question 'What are you hoping to achieve?' to come up with the aim.

> **Tip**
>
> The shared outcome should be suitable for the aim. For example, a presentation is a suitable way of persuading young people not to drop litter.

Main activity

Use this grid to draft the content of your shared outcome.

Topic:	
Shared outcome:	
Aim:	
First draft of shared outcome (use an additional sheet of paper if needed)	

Independent reflection activity

What was your best idea today?

....

How have you used communication skills today?

....

Check your learning

If you haven't already done so, complete the **How will I know if I reach my goals?** table with 'Not there yet' or 'Achieved'. Don't forget to add examples from your challenge.

6

Developing collaboration skills: Lesson 6

5.1 The team assign roles and divide tasks fairly, considering the skills of team members and time available, and work together to achieve a shared outcome

5.2 The team member introduces useful ideas to help achieve a shared outcome and works positively to resolve conflict, solve issues and encourage other team members to participate, when required

My learning goals are to develop my knowledge and understanding about:

- collaborating to produce shared outcomes
- how feedback can improve shared outcomes

How will I know if I reach my goals?

As you work through this lesson and you achieve your learning goals, tick the 'Achieved' box to show you have completed this. If you haven't quite achieved your learning goals, tick 'Not there yet'. Start to think about how you are going to show your learning goals in your challenge. Add an example from your challenge once you have achieved each learning goal.

Lesson 6	Not there yet	Achieved	Example
I can collaborate to produce a shared outcome.			
I can use feedback to improve a shared outcome.			
I can give feedback to improve a shared outcome.			

Prior learning

1   Why do you think it's important to gain feedback about any work that you have completed? Discuss with a partner.

....

2   Share your thoughts with your team members. Do they agree?   Yes/No

What other ideas do your team members have?

....

....

The topic I am working on today is …

....

Starter activity

Look at the document your teacher shows you.

1   What positive feedback would you give?

   Highlight 1

   ....

   ....

   Highlight 2

   ....

   ....

2   What helpful feedback would you give?

   Area for improvement

   ....

   ....

Class discussion

3   Using what you've learnt from class discussion, complete this sentence.

   Feedback is important because ....

   ....

   ....

   ....

   ....

Tip

When giving feedback, remember you are judging someone else's work, so try to praise the good things and be sensitive when explaining areas for improvement.

Tip

When giving feedback, focus on the work and be kind but honest, e.g. 'There was a claim, but I couldn't find any reasoning to justify this claim.'

Tip

Give helpful examples to allow for improvements, such as: 'Try to use less/more . . .'

Main activity

Peer feedback

1   Give feedback on the outcome that another team produced in Lesson 5.

2   On a separate piece of paper, create a final version of your own shared outcome, using the following headings: topic, aim, final shared outcome. Remember to include any feedback you received for your draft.

Independent reflection activity

I used to think that working as a team ....

....

Now I think ....

....

This is because ....

....

Example ....

....

Check your learning

If you haven't already done so, complete the **How will I know if I reach my goals?** table with 'Not there yet' or 'Achieved'. Don't forget to add examples from your challenge.

Self-assessment 2

Look back at self-assessment 1. How much further progress do you feel you have made so far in developing your collaboration skills?

For each learning objective in the table below, shade in the response that matches yours most closely. Give one example for this response. Eventually, you are aiming for green!

Learning objectives: *to develop my knowledge and understanding about how . . .*	RED	AMBER	GREEN
5.1 The team assign roles and divide tasks fairly, considering the skills of team members and time available, and work together to achieve a shared outcome.	I know what some of my strengths and skills are. I can give examples for some of my strengths and some of my teammates' strengths with help.	I know what some of my strengths and skills are. I can give examples for some of my strengths and skills and some of my teammates' strengths and skills. With help, I can give examples for ways I can develop my collaboration skills.	I know what my strengths and skills are. I can give examples for some of my strengths and skills and some of my teammates' strengths and skills. I can explain what effective teamwork is. I can give examples for ways I can develop my collaboration skills.
5.2 The team member introduces useful ideas to help achieve a shared outcome and works positively to resolve conflict, solve issues and encourage other team members to participate, when required.	I can share relevant ideas with others. I can explain how my contributions help towards planning and producing a shared outcome with help. I can suggest some ways of resolving conflict with help.	I can share relevant ideas with others. I can explain how my contributions help towards planning and producing a shared outcome. I can suggest some ways of resolving some conflict. I can encourage team members to participate.	I can share relevant ideas with others. I can explain how all team members' contributions help towards planning and producing a shared outcome. I can suggest ways of resolving different types of conflict. I can motivate and encourage team members to participate.

Continued

Examples:

5.1 ....

5.2 ....

Reflect on your responses in your self-assessment and identify two areas for improvement. Set yourself two learning targets – how you will improve upon the two areas. For example, 'I will practice taking my turn to speak to avoid conflict.'

Learning targets:

1   Area for improvement: ....

    How I will improve: ....

2   Area for improvement: ....

    How I will improve: ....

Challenge topic review

Think about the challenge topic you have been exploring and complete the following statements.

I was surprised to discover that ....

I didn't know ....

I now think ....

Getting better at collaboration skills: Lesson 7

5.1 The team assign roles and divide tasks fairly, considering the skills of team members and time available, and work together to achieve a shared outcome

5.2 The team member introduces useful ideas to help achieve a shared outcome and works positively to resolve conflict, solve issues and encourage other team members to participate, when required

---

My learning goals are to get better at:

- understanding what effective teamwork is
- reflecting on roles and responsibilities during teamwork
- evaluating teamwork

How will I know if I reach my goals?

As you work through this lesson and you achieve your learning goals, tick the 'Achieved' box to show you have completed this. If you haven't quite achieved your learning goals, tick 'Not there yet'. Start to think about how you are going to show your learning goals in your challenge. Add an example from your challenge once you have achieved each learning goal.

Lesson 7	Not there yet	Achieved	Example
I can give some examples for effective teamwork.			
I can identify the roles and responsibilities of team members during teamwork.			
I can identify strengths and areas that need improving in teamwork.			

Prior learning

1 What skill(s) did you use during teamwork in Lessons 3–6?

....

....

....

....

2 How did you use it/them?

....

....

....

....

Continued

3 Share examples with your team. Do you agree with the skill(s) they think they used and how they used it/them? Why? Complete the table.

Team member	Skill(s) identified	Agree Yes/No	Reason(s)

The topic I am working on today is …

....

Starter activity

1 Your teacher is going to give you a document entitled 'Effective teams'. Predict three features that you think will be in the text.

1 ....

2 ....

3 ....

2 Check your features from task **1** with the text. Did you predict accurately?

1 ....

2 ....

3 ....

3 Give an example of each feature from your own teamwork during Lessons 3–6.

1 ....

2 ....

3 ....

4 What do you think are the characteristics of ineffective teamwork?

....

....

....

Main activity

1 Complete the table to show how well each team member performed their role in the team.

> **Tip**
>
> Being honest when reflecting on your contribution to teamwork allows for improvements in future teamwork.

> **Tip**
>
> Reflecting on the contributions of others sometimes allows them to gain a different opinion to help them improve.

> **Tip**
>
> You are just starting to work in a team, so it doesn't matter that it wasn't perfect. All feedback is useful for development.

> **Tip**
>
> 'There is no "I" in 'TEAM' is an easy way to remember what teamwork is.

Use 😃 , 🙂 and 😐 for each role for each team member.

Team member role	Team members				
	Me				
Participated in team discussions					
Helped to keep the team on task					
Contributed useful/ relevant ideas					
Helped to resolve conflict(s)					
Helped to feed back on/review shared outcome					
Helped to complete shared outcome after feedback					

2 Complete the following table to show how you all worked together as a team to produce your shared outcome.

	YES	NO
Topic:		
Shared outcome:		
Team members:		
We finished our shared outcome on time.		
We did a good job on our shared outcome.		
We used quiet voices when we communicated.		
We each shared our ideas.		
We listened and valued each other's contributions.		

We did best at:
Next time, we need to improve on:

Independent reflection activity

What skill(s) have you improved today?

....

....

How did you improve it/them?

....

....

What skill(s) do you need to focus on improving?

....

....

Why?

....

....

Check your learning

If you haven't already done so, complete the **How will I know if I reach my goals?** table with 'Not there yet' or 'Achieved'. Don't forget to add examples from your challenge.

Self-assessment 3

Look back at self-assessments 1 and 2. How much further progress do you feel you have made so far in developing your collaboration skills?

For each learning objective in the table below, shade in the response that matches yours most closely. Give one example for this response.

Learning objectives: *to get better at understanding how . . .*	RED	AMBER	GREEN
5.1 The team assign roles and divide tasks fairly, considering the skills of team members and time available, and work together to achieve a shared outcome.	I know what some of my strengths and skills are. I can give examples for some of my strengths and some of my teammates' strengths with help. I can identify a skill that needs improving with help.	I know what some of my strengths and skills are. I can give examples for some of my strengths and skills and some of my teammates' strengths and skills. I can identify a skill that needs improving.	I know what my strengths and skills are. I can give examples for some of my strengths and skills and some of my teammates' strengths and skills. I can explain what effective teamwork is. I can identify skills I need to improve and say how I will do this.
5.2 The team member introduces useful ideas to help achieve a shared outcome and works positively to resolve conflict, solve issues and encourage other team members to participate, when required.	I can share relevant ideas with others. I can explain how my contributions helped towards planning and producing a shared outcome with help. I know at least one way of resolving conflict.	I can share relevant ideas with others. I can explain how my contributions helped towards planning and producing a shared outcome. I can suggest some ways of resolving conflict. I think I can encourage team members to participate.	I can share relevant ideas with others. I can explain how all team members' contributions helped towards planning and producing a shared outcome. I can suggest ways of resolving different types of conflict. I know I am able to motivate and encourage team members to participate.

Continued

Examples:

5.1 ....

5.2 ....

Reflect on your responses in your self-assessment and identify two areas for improvement. Set yourself two learning targets – how you will improve upon the two areas. For example, 'I will try to improve my ability to encourage and motivate other team members.'

Learning targets:

1   Area for improvement: ....

    How I will improve: ....

2   Area for improvement: ....

    How I will improve: ....

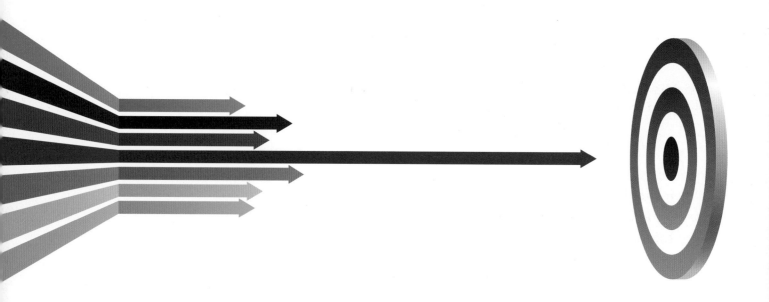

Communication

This section of your Learner's Skills Book 8 helps you to develop your communication skills using interesting global topics.

Starting with . . .

As you start to develop your communication skills in Stage 8, you will be learning to explain the term 'communication' and give examples of how you communicate in Global Perspectives lessons. You will explore how texts are structured and how you should structure a text to enable easy reading. You will also explore the different features of texts, both written and spoken, so that you can start to write your own well-structured arguments.

Developing . . .

As you further develop your communication skills in Stage 8, you will develop your understanding about how feedback is important to improve work. You will give and receive feedback based on specific criteria. You will be listening to and recording the ideas of others. As part of good communication, you will investigate what it means to listen actively, as opposed to passively, to clarify your understanding of an issue.

Getting better at . . .

As you get better at communicating with others in Stage 8, you will be exploring how best to present information that is clear and reasoned, and you will share your ideas with others so that they can also further develop their communication skills.

Starting with communication skills: Lesson 1

6.1 Present information and arguments clearly with some reasoning, referencing sources where appropriate

6.2 Listen to ideas and information and offer relevant and well-judged contributions that demonstrate understanding of the issue

How will I know if I reach my goals?

As you work through this lesson and you achieve your learning goals, tick the 'Achieved' box to show you have completed this. If you haven't quite achieved your learning goals, tick 'Not there yet'. Start to think about how you are going to show your learning goals in your challenge. Add an example from your challenge once you have achieved each learning goal.

Lesson 1	Not there yet	Achieved	Example
I can explain what communication is.			
I can give some examples of communication in Global Perspectives lessons.			
I can explain how to structure a text.			

Prior learning

1   Discuss with a partner. What does the term 'communication' mean to you?

    ....

    ....

2   Give some examples of how you communicate in Global Perspectives lessons.

    ....

    ....

    ....

3   Share examples with your classmates. Add two further examples of how you communicate in Global Perspectives lessons.

    ....

    ....

Starter activity

1   Structure is an important part of all written communication.
    When thinking about the structure of any text, which of these
    features do you think is important? Discuss the list with a partner.
    Number the statements in order, with 1 being most important and
    10 being least important.

A   The text contains understandable words and phrases.   ....

B   There is a beginning.   ....

C   The beginning introduces the main message.   ....

D   The end draws together the points made.   ....

E   There are paragraphs.   ....

F   Each point follows on from the next.   ....

G   There is a middle.   ....

H   There is a heading/title.   ....

I   Words and phrases are spelt correctly.   ....

J   There is a reference list.   ....

Peer feedback

2   Do your classmates agree? You can change your order in a different
    colour if you want to. Add one further feature to the list and say
    why you think it's important.

    ....

3   Discuss your list with a partner.
    Why is it important that texts have structure?

    ....

Class discussion

4   After class discussion, explain in your own words the best way to
    structure a text.

    ....

    ....

> **Tip**
>
> Text structure is
> about how the
> text is organised
> so that the reader
> can follow it
> easily.

The topic I am working on today is …

....

Main activity

1 Look at the text your teacher shows you. Discuss the following questions with your group, then note down your responses.

   a What is the main message in the text?

      ....

   b How many paragraphs are there?
      What is the key idea in each paragraph?

      ....

      ....

   c Do the ideas in each paragraph follow on from each other? Give an example.

      ....

      ....

   d Is there a conclusion? If so, does the conclusion sum up the points made in the rest of the text?

      ....

> **Tip**
>
> In Global Perspectives, a conclusion is important to reflect on your own personal perspective about the issue after exploring the causes, consequences and different perspectives.

   e Is there a heading/title? Does this relate to the content of the text?

      ....

> **Tip**
>
> Global Perspectives texts are usually made up of a beginning (introduction linked to the heading/title/research question), a middle (main points: claims, reasoning and evidence) and an end (conclusion summing up the evidence and reflecting on personal perspective).

> **Tip**
>
> For Global Perspectives, a paragraph will present a claim, reasoning to justify the claim and evidence to support the claim.

f Is there a reference list? If so, is it accurate?

....

g Do you understand all the words and phrases?
Are they spelt correctly?

....

h Do you think this text is well-structured? Yes/No

Why? ....

Class discussion

2 Using what you have learnt from class discussion, add any further ideas to your responses to **a–h** in a different colour.

Independent reflection activity

What did you learn about text structure today that you haven't previously considered?

....

What skill(s) did you use today?

....

How?

....

Check your learning

If you haven't already done so, complete the **How will I know if I reach my goals?** table with 'Not there yet' or 'Achieved'. Don't forget to add examples from your challenge.

Starting with communication skills: Lesson 2

6.1 Present information and arguments clearly with some reasoning, referencing sources where appropriate

6.2 Listen to ideas and information and offer relevant and well-judged contributions that demonstrate understanding of the issue

My learning goals are to start to:

- explain what helps to make a well-structured argument

- create a well-structured argument with a claim, reasoning and supporting evidence

- contribute ideas to show understanding of an issue

How will I know if I reach my goals?

As you work through this lesson and you achieve your learning goals, tick the 'Achieved' box to show you have completed this. If you haven't quite achieved your learning goals, tick 'Not there yet'. Start to think about how you are going to show your learning goals in your challenge. Add an example from your challenge once you have achieved each learning goal.

Lesson 2	Not there yet	Achieved	Example
I can explain what helps to make a well-structured argument.			
I can create a well-structured argument with a claim, reasoning and supporting evidence.			
I can contribute ideas to show understanding of an issue.			

Prior learning

1 Select the 5 most important features to make a well-structured argument. Mark these with a tick.

	Features	✓		Features	✓
1	conclusion		9	reasoning	
2	different perspectives		10	reference list	
3	Paragraphs		11	title/heading	
4	punctuation		12	supporting evidence	
5	middle		13	relevant words and phrases	
6	claims		14	sub-headings	
7	makes sense		15	transition words	
8	beginning				

2 Discuss the elements with your partner. Which ones do you and your partner agree on?

....

3 Why do you think these elements are important?

....

The topic I am working on today is …

....

Starter activity

1   Look at the sub-topic your teacher gives you. Discuss it with a partner. Write down three claims that might be appropriate to the sub-topic.

1   ....

2   ....

3   ....

2   Find another pair with the same sub-topic. Discuss all the claims. As a group, choose one claim to create an argument in the Main activity.

....

Main activity

Use your chosen claim from the Starter activity. As a group, research and record your ideas for an argument for your claim in this table.

Claim:	
Introduction	

Tip

A claim is an assertion that something is true.

Tip

The introduction should make it clear what the argument is about and link to your title and claim.

Tip

The middle will be made up of more than one paragraph. Each paragraph will include evidence to support the claim(s) made.

Middle	
Conclusion	

Independent reflection activity

How did you learn best today?

....

How did you help someone else learn today?

....

What skill(s) did you use or improve today? How?

....

....

Check your learning

If you haven't already done so, complete the **How will I know if I reach my goals?** table with 'Not there yet' or 'Achieved'. Don't forget to add examples from your challenge.

3

Starting with communication skills: Lesson 3

6.1 Present information and arguments clearly with some reasoning, referencing sources where appropriate

6.2 Listen to ideas and information and offer relevant and well-judged contributions that demonstrate understanding of the issue

My learning goals are to start to:

- explain the features that help to create a well-structured argument
- create a well-structured argument with a claim, reasoning and supporting evidence
- give and receive feedback to improve an argument

How will I know if I reach my goals?

As you work through this lesson and you achieve your learning goals, tick the 'Achieved' box to show you have completed this. If you haven't quite achieved your learning goals, tick 'Not there yet'. Start to think about how you are going to show your learning goals in your challenge. Add an example from your challenge once you have achieved each learning goal.

Lesson 3	Not there yet	Achieved	Example
I know some features that help create a well-structured argument in Global Perspectives.			
I can create a well-structured argument, with a claim, reasoning and supporting evidence.			
I can give and receive feedback to improve an argument.			

Prior learning

1   What features help create a well-structured argument in Global Perspectives?

1 ....

2 ....

3 ....

2   Using what you've learnt from class discussion, add two further features.

4 ....

5 ....

The topic I am working on today is ...

....

Starter activity

1　Work in the same group from Lesson 2. Review the notes for your argument from the Main activity in Lesson 2.

2　Add any further ideas.

Main activity

1　Write the script for your argument.

Claim:	
Introduction	
Middle	
Conclusion	

> **Tip**
>
> You should start a new paragraph when you begin a new idea or point; to compare information; and when you are ending your introduction or starting your conclusion.

> **Tip**
>
> When referring to evidence in an argument, use transition words such as 'for example'; 'for instance'; 'to demonstrate'.

> **Tip**
>
> When writing the conclusion of an argument, use transition words such as 'Finally'; 'In conclusion'; 'To sum up'; 'As you can see'.

2　As a team, discuss your script and make any amendments necessary.

3 Check your script by completing the table.

Claim: ....
Title: ....

Is/are there . . . ?	Yes	No	Notes
an introduction (including title)			
a conclusion (including personal perspective)			
a middle with claims			
reasoning to justify the claims in the middle			
supporting evidence for the claims in the middle			
a reference list			
transition words/ phrases (e.g. 'therefore', 'so', 'in summary')			
accurate spelling			

Tip

When giving feedback, always start with the positive and give more positives than negatives.

Is/are there . . . ?	Yes	No	Notes
relevant topic-specific words and phrases			
punctuation			
paragraphs			
different perspectives			
a logical structure			

Tip

Be prepared to give an example for any points you make that will help improve someone else's work.

Tip

Remember that good feedback is not personal; it's about the work produced.

Peer feedback

4   Give feedback to another team on their script using the table in task **3**.

Independent reflection activity

Which skill did you improve this lesson?

....

How did you improve it?

....

Which skill do you still need to work on?

....

Check your learning

If you haven't already done so, complete the **How will I know if I reach my goals?** table with 'Not there yet' or 'Achieved'. Don't forget to add examples from your challenge.

Self-assessment 1

How much progress do you feel you have made so far in developing your communication skills?

For each learning objective in the table below, shade in the response that matches yours most closely. Give one example for this response. Eventually, you are aiming for green!

Learning objectives: to start to . . .	RED	AMBER	GREEN
6.1 Present information and arguments clearly with some reasoning, referencing sources where appropriate.	I understand what communication is. I can give some examples of communication in Global Perspectives with help. I can explain at least one feature of a well-structured argument with help. I can write a paragraph, including a claim, some reasoning and at least one piece of evidence with help.	I understand what communication is. I can give some examples of communication in Global Perspectives. I can explain some features of a well-structured argument. I can write a paragraph, including a claim, some reasoning and some evidence.	I understand what communication is. I can help others give examples of communication in Global Perspectives. I can explain some features of a well-structured argument and help others recognise these. I can write a paragraph. including a claim, some reasoning and some evidence and I can help others identify well-structured paragraphs.
6.2 Listen to ideas and information and offer relevant and well-judged contributions that demonstrate understanding of the issue.	I can listen and identify some key ideas and information with help. I can share some ideas with others, although they may not always be relevant or well-judged.	I can listen and identify some key ideas and information. I can share relevant ideas with others, some of which show my understanding of a topic/an issue.	I can listen and identify some key ideas and information. I can share relevant ideas that show my understanding of a topic/an issue with others. I can help others understand an issue/a topic.

Continued

Examples:

6.1 ....

6.2 ....

Reflect on your responses in your self-assessment and identify two areas for improvement. Set yourself two learning targets – how you will improve upon the two areas. For example, 'I need to make sure that I support my claims with at least one piece of evidence.'

Learning targets:

1   Area for improvement: ....

    How I will improve: ....

2   Area for improvement: ....

    How I will improve: ....

Challenge topic review

Think about the challenge topic you have been exploring and complete the following statements.

I was surprised to discover that ....

I didn't know ....

I now think ....

Developing communication skills: Lesson 4

6.1 Present information and arguments clearly with some reasoning, referencing sources where appropriate

6.2 Listen to ideas and information and offer relevant and well-judged contributions that demonstrate understanding of the issue

My learning goals are to develop my knowledge and understanding about:

- the importance of feedback
- listening to and recording ideas and information gained from others

How will I know if I reach my goals?

As you work through this lesson and you achieve your learning goals, tick the 'Achieved' box to show you have completed this. If you haven't quite achieved your learning goals, tick 'Not there yet'. Start to think about how you are going to show your learning goals in your challenge. Add an example from your challenge once you have achieved each learning goal.

Lesson 4	Not there yet	Achieved	Example
I understand the importance of giving and receiving feedback.			
I can listen and record relevant ideas and information gained from others.			

Prior learning

Discuss the following questions with your team.

1   Why is feedback important?

    ....

    ....

2   What do you need to remember when giving feedback?

    ....

    ....

The topic I am working on today is …

....

Starter activity

1   Discuss the feedback given to your team on your argument in Lesson 3.

2   As a team, improve your script using the feedback.

3   Get ready to read your argument or record it as a podcast.

Main activity

1   Listen to another team's argument, making notes to complete the table.

Claim:			
Title:			
Is/are there . . . ?	Yes	No	Notes
an introduction (including title)			
a conclusion (including personal perspective)			
a middle with claims			
reasoning to justify the claims in the middle			
supporting evidence for the claims in the middle			
transition words/phrases (e.g. 'therefore', 'so', 'in summary')			
relevant topic-specific words and phrases			
different perspectives			
a logical structure			

Peer feedback

2 Give overall feedback to the other team on their argument.

Claim:	
Title:	
Team:	
☆	
☆	
☆	

Independent reflection activity

Which part of today's lesson helped you learn most? Why?

....

....

On a scale of 1–10, with 10 being the most, what effort did you put into today's lesson? Give a reason why you have scored yourself this number.

My effort in today's lesson									
1	2	3	4	5	6	7	8	9	10

Reason(s): ....

....

Check your learning

If you haven't already done so, complete the **How will I know if I reach my goals?** table with 'Not there yet' or 'Achieved'. Don't forget to add examples from your challenge.

5

Developing communication skills: Lesson 5

6.1 Present information and arguments clearly with some reasoning, referencing sources where appropriate

6.2 Listen to ideas and information and offer relevant and well-judged contributions that demonstrate understanding of the issue

My learning goals are to develop my knowledge and understanding about:

- presenting information clearly
- recording information accurately
- listening actively to increase understanding

How will I know if I reach my goals?

As you work through this lesson and you achieve your learning goals, tick the 'Achieved' box to show you have completed this. If you haven't quite achieved your learning goals, tick 'Not there yet'. Start to think about how you are going to show your learning goals in your challenge. Add an example from your challenge once you have achieved each learning goal.

Lesson 5	Not there yet	Achieved	Example
I can present information clearly.			
I can record information accurately.			
I can listen actively to increase my understanding of an issue.			

Prior learning

1   How do you know when someone is listening actively? Discuss with a partner.

....

....

....

2   Do your classmates agree? Using what you've learnt from class discussion, add further ideas in a different colour.

The topic I am working on today is …

....

Starter activity

1   Look at the picture your teacher gives you. Describe it to your partner without showing them the picture, so that they can sketch it or write notes on what it contains

2 Now it's your turn to listen.
Then sketch or write notes about your partner's picture.

Topic/sub-topic of picture:
Details (notes or sketch):

3 Did you include all the details in your partner's picture?　　Yes/No

4 Why do you think this was?

....

5 What did you find challenging about this activity? Why?

....

....

Main activity

1 Watch or listen actively to the video/audio clips your teacher plays.
Then complete the table.

	Main message	Other information
1		

Tip

Active listening is about attentively trying to understand what someone says rather than passively hearing the words that someone says.

Tip

When presenting information, it's important that you speak clearly and slowly and give as many details as you can.

Tip

Show that you are listening actively by giving verbal and non-verbal feedback. This shows you are really interested in what someone is saying.

2		
3		

Tip

Non-verbal feedback includes nodding, leaning forward and making eye contact.

Tip

Verbal feedback includes affirmations like 'I see', 'I know', 'Sure' and 'I understand'.

Peer feedback

2   Share your ideas with a partner. Add further ideas in a different colour.

3   Share your ideas with another pair. Add further ideas in a different colour.

4   Look at your completed table. Did you find out much information from your classmates?   Yes/No

5   How do you think sharing and listening to the ideas of others helps you?

   ....

Independent reflection activity

How do you know that you've been actively listening?

....

What other skills have you used today? How?

....

....

Check your learning

If you haven't already done so, complete the **How will I know if I reach my goals?** table with 'Not there yet' or 'Achieved'. Don't forget to add examples from your challenge.

Developing communication skills: Lesson 6

6.1 Present information and arguments clearly with some reasoning, referencing sources where appropriate

6.2 Listen to ideas and information and offer relevant and well-judged contributions that demonstrate understanding of the issue

My learning goals are to develop my knowledge and understanding about:

- presenting information clearly and with some reasoning

- improving listening skills to gain information

How will I know if I reach my goals?

As you work through this lesson and you achieve your learning goals, tick the 'Achieved' box to show you have completed this. If you haven't quite achieved your learning goals, tick 'Not there yet'. Start to think about how you are going to show your learning goals in your challenge. Add an example from your challenge once you have achieved each learning goal.

Lesson 6	Not there yet	Achieved	Example
I can present information clearly with some reasoning.			
I can listen actively to gain information.			

Prior learning

Complete the following:

Giving feedback helps ....

Receiving feedback helps ....

When giving feedback, we should remember ....

When receiving feedback, we should remember ....

The topic I am working on today is …

....

Starter activity

Listen and write down the statements your teacher reads. Answer with true (T) or false (F) .

1 ....

2 ....

3 ....

Tip

When clarifying information, always check the details are the same on more than one website. This is called cross-referencing.

4 ....

5 ....

6 ....

7 ....

8 ....

9 ....

10 ....

Tip

The type of information you find depends on the type of website, e.g. a blog will give someone's opinion, whereas a scientific report will report facts.

Main activity

1 Do some research on the statements from the Starter activity.
   Correct your answers if necessary.

2 Use this table to record evidence to support your answers.
   For each statement that was false, write a new true statement.

	T/F	Website address	True statements (if needed)
1			
2			
3			
4			
5			
6			
7			

	T/F	Website address	True statements (if needed)
8			
9			
10			

3 Discuss and create five new statements with a partner.
Ask another pair if the statements are true or false.

	Statements	T/F
11		
12		
13		
14		
15		

Independent reflection activity

I used to think ....

Now I think ....

This is because ....

....

Check your learning

If you haven't already done so, complete the **How will I know if I reach my goals?** table
with 'Not there yet' or 'Achieved'. Don't forget to add examples from your challenge.

Self-assessment 2

Look back at self-assessment 1. How much further progress do you feel you have made so far in developing your communication skills?

For each learning objective in the table below, shade in the response that matches yours most closely. Give one example for this response. Eventually, you are aiming for green!

Learning objectives: *to develop my knowledge and understanding about how to …*	RED	AMBER	GREEN
6.1 Present information and arguments clearly with some reasoning, referencing sources where appropriate.	I understand what communication is. I know why it is important to give and receive feedback. I can give some feedback to improve arguments with help. I can present some information with some reasoning with help.	I understand what communication is. I know why it is important to give and receive feedback. I can give some feedback to improve arguments. I can present some information clearly with some reasoning.	I understand what communication is. I know why it is important to give and receive feedback. I can give feedback to improve arguments and help others give feedback. I can present information clearly with some reasoning and help others with reasoning.
6.2 Listen to ideas and information and offer relevant and well-judged contributions that demonstrate understanding of the issue.	I can listen and record some key ideas and information with help. I can share some ideas with others, although the ideas may not always be relevant or well-judged or might not always show my understanding of an issue.	I can listen and record some key ideas and information. I can share with others some ideas, which sometimes show my understanding of an issue.	I can listen and record key ideas and information and help others to identify key information. I can share with others ideas that clearly show my understanding of an issue.

Continued

Examples:

6.1 ....

6.2 ....

Reflect on your responses in your self-assessment and identify two areas for improvement. Set yourself two learning targets – how you will improve upon the two areas. For example, 'I will try not to get distracted when listening.'

Learning targets:

1 Area for improvement: ....

   How I will improve: ....

2 Area for improvement: ....

   How I will improve: ....

Challenge topic review

Think about the challenge topic you have been exploring and complete the following statements.

I was surprised to discover that ....

I didn't know ....

I now think ....

7

Getting better at communication skills: Lesson 7

6.1 Present information and arguments clearly with some reasoning, referencing sources where appropriate

6.2 Listen to ideas and information and offer relevant and well-judged contributions that demonstrate understanding of the issue

My learning goals are to get better at:

- presenting information with reasoning
- sharing ideas with others

How will I know if I reach my goals?

As you work through this lesson and you achieve your learning goals, tick the 'Achieved' box to show you have completed this. If you haven't quite achieved your learning goals, tick 'Not there yet'. Start to think about how you are going to show your learning goals in your challenge. Add an example from your challenge once you have achieved each learning goal.

Lesson 7	Not there yet	Achieved	Example
I can present information with some reasoning.			
I can share relevant ideas and information with others.			

Prior learning

1 What skills have you been developing throughout your Global Perspectives lessons?

....

....

....

2 Share examples with your classmates.

....

....

....

The topic I am working on today is …

....

Starter activity

1 Look at the picture(s) your teacher shows you.
Complete the first two columns below.

What I know about the picture	What I want to know about it	What I have learnt

Class discussion

2   Using what you've learnt from class discussion, add to the first two columns.

3   Do some research to complete the third column.

Main activity

1   Using the information from the Starter activity and/or information you have gained about the topic in previous lessons, use a separate piece of paper to create an outcome to raise awareness about one of the issues to do with the topic. The outcome can be a rap, song or poem. Add references to say where you got your information from.

2   Share your outcome with your classmates.

3   Decide which teams presented the best three outcomes and why.

a   Team ....

because ....

b   Team ....

because ....

c   Team ....

because ....

> **Tip**
>
> When presenting information, use short sentences. Short sentences help people remember the key message.

> **Tip**
>
> As well as presentations and video clips, raps, songs and poems can be creative outcomes to raise awareness about issues.

Independent reflection activity

Which skill did you improve today?

....

How did you improve this skill?

....

What skill(s) do you still need to improve?

....

Check your learning

If you haven't already done so, complete the **How will I know if I reach my goals?** table with 'Not there yet' or 'Achieved'. Don't forget to add examples from your challenge.

Self-assessment 3

Look back at self-assessments 1 and 2. How much further progress do you feel you have made so far in developing your communication skills?

For each learning objective in the table below, shade in the response that matches yours most closely. Give one example for this response. Eventually, you are aiming for green!

Learning objectives: *to get better at understanding how to ...*	RED	AMBER	GREEN
6.1 Present information and arguments clearly with some reasoning, referencing sources where appropriate.	I understand what communication is. I know why it is important to give and receive feedback. I can give some feedback to improve arguments with help. I can present some information clearly with some reasoning with help.	I understand what communication is. I know why it is important to give and receive feedback. I can give some feedback to improve arguments. I can present some information clearly with some reasoning.	I understand what communication is. I know why it is important to give and receive feedback. I can give feedback to improve arguments and can help others give feedback. I can present information clearly with some reasoning and can help others with reasoning.
6.2 Listen to ideas and information and offer relevant and well-judged contributions that demonstrate understanding of the issue.	I can listen and record some key ideas and information with help. I can share some ideas with others, although the ideas may not always be relevant or well-judged or might not always show my understanding of an issue.	I can listen and record some key ideas and information. I can share with others some ideas, which sometimes show my understanding of an issue.	I can listen and record key ideas and information and help others to identify key information. I can share with others ideas that clearly show my understanding of an issue.

Continued

Examples:

6.1 ....

6.2 ....

Reflect on your responses in your self-assessment and identify two areas for improvement. Set yourself two learning targets – how you will improve upon the two areas. For example, 'When I work with others, I will listen to their ideas before I share mine'.

Learning targets:

1 Area for improvement: ....

   How I will improve: ....

2 Area for improvement: ....

   How I will improve: ....

Challenge topic review

Think about the challenge topic you have been exploring and complete the following statements.

I was surprised to discover that ....

I didn't know ....

I now think ....

Glossary

active listening	attentively trying to understand what someone says rather than passively hearing the words
aim	the purpose of a shared outcome
analysis	breaking down a global topic into issues and exploring causes and consequences of these issues
argument	consists of a claim, the reasons for that claim and evidence to support the claim
bias	a judgment based on a personal point of view, which may be unfair or could favour or be prejudiced against a certain side
cause	the reason(s) why an event or situation happens
cite	to refer to a text, book or author as evidence to help support an argument
claim	a statement or an assertion that something is true
closed question	a question that often has a yes/no or specific answer; often prompted by 'what' questions
collaboration	working together with others
communication	a way to transfer information from one place to another, usually by speaking and writing
compromise	to reach common agreement
conclusion	sums up points made in a text
consequence	the result or effect of something that has happened
double bar graph	a bar graph that compares two sets of data
evaluation	identifying strengths and limitations/weaknesses
evidence	anything that can support or back up a claim
fact	something that can be proven to be true
fake news	false information deliberately created to trick people into believing it is true
feedback	giving information to someone about something
global perspective	thinking about a situation or issue as it relates to the whole world
issue	an important topic/sub-topic or problem for debate or discussion
limitation	usually something that is lacking or not done very well
local perspective	thinking about a situation or issue as it relates to a specific region or locality
national perspective	thinking about a situation or issue as it relates to a specific country
non-verbal feedback	feedback that is not spoken, including nodding, leaning forward and making eye contact
one-sided argument	an argument that does not present all the evidence
opinion	a viewpoint/idea that cannot be proven
open-ended question	a question requiring a longer answer than yes/no; often prompted by 'why' or 'how'

outcome	a product to achieve a specific aim.
paragraph	usually presents a claim, reasoning and evidence
personal perspective	what an individual thinks about a topic/issue as a result of research findings
personal strength	something an individual is good at
perspective	a certain world view or way of looking at something
prediction	a statement about what might happen in the future
primary research	the method for collecting data that has not been collected before and is collected directly from individuals, groups of people or research observations
questionnaire	a way of gaining different opinions/viewpoints to help develop a perspective, usually a local perspective about an issue, often referred to as a primary source of information as responses are given directly to the person who wrote the questionnaire
reasoning	justification for something, e.g. a claim or argument, often introduced by 'because …'
reference	details of a source of information, including the author, title, publication date, any website address and date the website was accessed
reference list	a list of all the sources of information researched and used in written work
reflection	to think hard about something
reflective learning	to think hard about what you are learning
reliable source of information	a source that can be trusted to be true
research	a way of collecting information
research question	a question that enables you to carry out research about a specific issue
search engine	a program on a computer that searches for and identifies suitable information
secondary research	the method of collecting data from existing/published sources of information
shared outcome	something produced as a team
source	a place from which information can be obtained to inform a person about something
stakeholder	someone with a vested interested in a topic/issue
teamwork	working with a group of people towards a shared outcome
text structure	how the text is organised so that the reader can follow it
topic-specific words	words that are related to a main idea/topic
transition words	words that help to link ideas together, e.g. 'Finally', 'As you can see'
unreliable source	a source that cannot be trusted to be true
verbal feedback	spoken feedback, including affirmations like 'I see', 'I know', 'Sure' and 'I understand'

> Acknowledgements

The authors and publishers acknowledge the following sources of copyright material and are grateful for the permissions granted.

Thanks to the following for permission to reproduce images:

Easyturn/Getty Images; Nancy Honey/Getty Images; kali9/Getty Images; 4FR/Getty Images/ Izabela Habur/Getty Images; Camille Tokerud Photography Inc./Getty Images/Getty Images; real444/Getty Images; Getty Images; KTSDESIGN/SCIENCE PHOTO LIBRARY/Getty Images; Panuwat Dangsungnoen/EyeEm/Getty Images; DMEPhotography/Getty Images/J/J Images-J Morrill Photo/Getty Images; jayk7/Getty Images; DjelicS/Getty Images/Shutterstock/ Colorlife; Fernando Trabanco Fotografía/Getty Images; portishead1/Getty Images/Getty Images; ljubaphoto/Getty Images; ViewStock/Getty Images; Virojt Changyencham/Getty Images; crispyicon/Getty Images; SDI Productions/Getty Images; Qi Yang/Getty Images/BFC/ Ascent Xmedia/Getty Images; NurPhoto/Getty Images; calvindexter/Getty Images/golero/Getty Images; MirageC/Getty Images; Constantine Johnny.Getty Images/krisanapong detraphiphat/Getty Images; Marco Canoniero/Getty Images/Education Images/Getty Images; NurPhoto/Getty Images; Nodar Chernishev / EyeEm/Getty Images/NurPhoto/Getty Images; Jeff Greenberg/Getty Images; krisanapong detraphiphat/Getty Images/Auscape/Getty Images; jayk7/Getty Images; wateye/Getty Images; Andrew Spencer/Getty Images/Mike Kemp/Getty Images; Peter Dazeley/ Getty Images; Thomas Lohnes/Getty Images/Mohamad Faizal Ramli / EyeEm/Getty Images; Hindustan Times/Getty Images/lvcandy/Getty Imges; Hindustan Times/Getty Images; alexsl/Getty Images/ARIEF BAGUS/Getty Images; Mondadori Portfolio/Getty Images; twomeows/Getty Images/Thomas Barwick/Getty Images; enviromantic/Getty Images; Eskay Lim / EyeEm/Getty Images/YASUYOSHI CHIBA/Getty Images; Keith Levit/Getty Images; SDI Productions/Getty Images/Jennifer A Smith/Getty Images; Hill Street Studios/Getty Images; fairywong/Getty Images/ Patrick Foto/Getty Images; DEA / V. GIANNELLA/Getty Images; Paula Daniëlse/Getty Images/ Hindustan Times/Getty Images; NurPhoto/Getty Images; Katja Kircher/Getty Images/jayk7/ Getty Images; Klaus Vedfelt/Getty Images; jayk7/Getty Images; Godong/Getty Images/TAUSEEF MUSTAFA/Getty Images; Education Images/Getty Images; Rick Loomis/Getty Images/jayk7/ Getty Images; Anadolu Agency/Getty Images; Francesco Carta fotografo/Getty Images/hh5800/ Getty Images; yimwow/Getty Images; lvcandy/Getty Images; Ariel Skelley/Getty Images/hh5800/ Getty Images; domin_domin/Getty Images; Drew Angerer/Getty Images/AFP/Getty Images; SDI Productions/Getty Images; Klaus Vedfelt/Getty Images/Marc Mcdermott / EyeEm/Getty Images; Hindustan Times/Getty Images; mikroman6/Hindustan Times/Getty Images; Christopher Furlong/Getty Images